"*(Extra)Ordinary Women: Ten Inspirational Stories* is a journey into the very marrow of which strong women are made. Kristin Bartzokis fearlessly weaves a well-told tapestry of strength and perseverance proving our struggles do not define us, but rather propel us to become the best version of ourselves. This book is a must-read for women and men of all ages."

—Joanie Cox-Henry, journalist and blogger

"The women of *Extraordinary Women* not only share in experiencing the kinds of adversity most of us fear, they share an indomitable resilience of spirit. Their stories must be told, their ordeals understood, because the human collective can only benefit from their power."

—Aimee Ross, author of *Permanent Marker: A Memoir*

"Kristin Bartzokis, known for her trailblazing memoir *Diary of a Beautiful Disaster*, reminds readers that how a person responds to adversity is what makes her extraordinary. The ten women featured come from a variety of backgrounds, and the beauty of unity in diversity is exemplified in each story. In each woman's story you are likely to find an aspect of her life to connect to your own."

— Sarah McCune, former director of communications for FACES: The National Craniofacial Association

(EXTRA)ORDINARY (WOMEN)

TEN INSPIRATIONAL STORIES

KRISTIN BARTZOKIS

Cover and book design by Mark Sullivan

ISBN 978-0-9991581-4-2 (paperback)
ISBN 978-0-9991581-5-9 (e-book)
Library of Congress Control Number: 2018947931

Printed in the United States of America

Published by KiCam Projects
www.KiCamProjects.com

Mom, this incredible life wouldn't have been possible without your constant strength and unwavering love.
(*hand squeeze, hand squeeze, hand squeeze*)

Contents

Introduction

What makes someone an inspiration to others? That is a question I asked myself a lot while growing up. Because I was born with Treacher Collins syndrome, people often told me *I* was an inspiration, but I never felt like one. I was just an ordinary person who handled her life of reconstructive surgeries with as much strength and courage as she could. What other choice did I have? I was simply living my life the way anyone would.

As I matured, I realized I had the ability to compartmentalize my life and not let my syndrome take control. I chose to see it as a piece of me, rather than the very thing that defined me. I not only accept my differences; I embrace them.

Today, I walk through life with the understanding that what makes someone an inspiration is not that she has accomplished a monumental feat; it is how she chooses to live her everyday life and overcome adversity. Being an inspiration doesn't mean you have to do something drastic or huge; it means you have found a way to face your obstacles in a manner that others will strive to emulate.

Each of us looks for a hero, whether we realize it or not. We find particular traits that we admire in others and then adopt them as our own. Sometimes this happens automatically because it's all we have ever been exposed to. I learned how to be strong from my mother. As she sat by my hospital bedside time and time again, I watched her stay composed in the most challenging situations. Witnessing her fortitude helped me find my own strength when I needed it most.

My story is not the only one with an influential mother. The mother-daughter relationship shines throughout the stories in this book. Many of these inspirational women are who they are today because of what they learned from their own mothers.

Each of the women in this book found a way to beat the odds stacked against her. Every one of these women proves that although we do not always have control of the situations in our lives, we can control how we react to those situations.

These women chose to learn from their most difficult moments. They chose to view their pain as an opportunity to make positive changes to their lives and become the best versions of themselves. They also chose to turn their pain into compassion, using their experiences to improve the lives of others.

In my opinion, that's what inspiration is all about: growing from your trials and choosing to make a difference.

This is a pivotal moment in history for women—a time to rise, unite, and show the world what we're made of. The women in this book remind us that even everyday acts of fearlessness and fortitude can leave a lasting impression for generations. I hope you find strength and empowerment in these chapters, just as I did.

Olga

Few Americans know that after World War II, Greece suffered through a terrible civil war, which brought more misery and bloodshed to a population that already had endured four years of hardship. In fact, post-World War II Greece was marked by a type of brutality that at times was comparable to, if not greater than, that of the sadistic Nazis. Olga Gatzoyiannis knew all of this far too well. The emotional scars she suffered as a result of the Greek Civil War never healed, and she continued to feel the effects of those scars throughout her life. (Olga passed away in January 2018, at age eighty-nine, while this book was being edited.)

In 1946, Communist insurgents in Greece rose up against the Western-aligned Greek government and sought to institute Communist rule throughout the country. Towns and villages in the northwest portion of Greece were particularly susceptible to the uprising, as they were bordered by two Communist countries, Albania and Yugoslavia. The tiny village of Lia, home to the Gatzoyiannis family, was situated in that area, only a few hundred yards from the Albanian border. In November 1947, Lia was overrun by Communist soldiers, effectively cutting off the village from the free world. Olga and her family became prisoners in their own village.

Before the war years, Olga had been very happy in her secluded mountainside home. She, her four younger siblings, and her mother lived in a small four-room house, where one room served as the bedroom for all. Olga's father lived in the United States, in Worcester, Massachusetts, where he worked various jobs, sending money back to his family whenever he could, hoping someday he could afford to bring them all to America to join him. But Olga knew any such move would be far off in the future, as her father was struggling to support even himself in the New World.

As a young girl, Olga passed her days working alongside her mother, Eleni, threshing wheat, tending the sheep and goats, cooking, cleaning, and keeping an eye on her siblings. As long as Olga had her mother nearby, she was happy. The two possessed a special bond, and Olga cherished that relationship.

During the early years of World War II, Lia was left pretty much untouched by the invading armies, its isolation being a deterrent to any military campaigns. But in early 1944, that all changed. The German army stormed into the village, seeking to flush out Greek partisan fighters. Olga trembled at the sight of the mighty army as it passed through her village, and she prayed the Germans would move on without incident. But when Greek resistance fighters hiding in the mountains took shots at the passing enemy troops, the German commander ordered an all-out retaliation. He instructed his soldiers to burn the village to the ground; no structure was to remain standing.

Most villagers, including Olga, fled to faraway places, high up in the mountains, in order to escape the wrath of the Germans, but one of Olga's aunts chose to stay behind. When her home was set on fire, she began to wail and scream. A nearby German officer told her to quiet down, but she was too distraught to stop. After several minutes of this "nuisance," the officer ordered his subordinates to throw her into the burning home. They picked her up, tossed her through an open window, and laughed as she screamed in agony for the next several seconds. Soon the noise faded away.

News of the brutal murder shocked the people of Lia, including Olga, who was particularly traumatized by the event because it involved one of her favorite aunts. She couldn't believe anyone could be so evil as to kill an old woman simply because she was crying. Unfortunately, Olga's lessons in brutality did not stop when the German threat ended the following year. In fact, the worst was yet to come.

After the Allied defeat of Germany in 1945, Olga expected her father to arrange for their move to America so they could all be together. Unfortunately, he was woefully short of funds and told his family they would have to stay in Greece a while longer. As of autumn 1947, the family was still in Greece, and by then, Communist insurgents had risen up throughout the country. When the insurgency arrived in Lia in November, whatever hope Olga had of escaping to America ended with the pronouncement by the Communist leaders that the village had been "liberated."

For Olga, liberation meant that guerrilla leaders confiscated her home. It also meant that her mother, Eleni, had to give them all the family's valuable possessions, as well as most of their food. Everyone in the family was required to work the fields so anything edible could be harvested for "the cause."

Life under the guerrillas was difficult for Olga. Her mother used all the resources available to her to keep the family fed, and although they weren't eating the way they had before the war, they were not starving. One day, however, Eleni learned that the older girls in the village were going to be conscripted into the army to become guerrilla fighters. They were going to be forced to carry guns and other weapons and fight as soldiers alongside the men.

Olga was horrified when she heard the news, knowing she would be taken. She had heard stories about how some young women conscripted by the Communists were raped and abused by the male soldiers, especially if they were believed to be sympathetic to the Greek government. "I knew I had to do something to keep from being taken," Olga recounted years later. "I would surely have been killed in battle or abused by the guerrillas if I went."

That night, Eleni told Olga she had an idea. It was the only way she could think of to keep Olga from being taken by the Communists the next day. It was a trick Greek women had used for centuries to keep their daughters out of harm's way. It would be painful, but if it worked, Olga would be safe. Olga was afraid but understood that whatever her mother had in mind needed to be done. "I knew what was coming," Olga admitted, "and I knew the pain would be like nothing I had ever experienced before."

When Eleni was ready, she called Olga over to the fireplace where she and Olga's maternal grandmother were seated. Eleni ordered her mother to hold Olga down as firmly as she could. Then, without warning, she poured a pot of boiling water over Olga's right leg. Olga let out a terrible scream. Eleni threw the pot away and looked at the leg to see if the boiling water had done its job. To her horror, it had not. Despite all the agony she had just put her daughter through, the leg did not appear disfigured. It was red in color and had a few blisters, but it was not grotesque and certainly would not impress the guerrilla officers when they came calling the next day. They would take her despite her injury. Olga's ordeal was not over yet.

Olga's grandmother quickly removed a hot poker from the fireplace and, again, without warning, pressed it against the side of Olga's right foot. The smell of burning flesh quickly filled the room, and Olga cried out. In a few seconds, the poker was removed. Skin clung to it as Olga's grandmother tossed the poker away. When she looked at Olga's ankle, she was appalled at what she saw; the poker had burned through to the bone, exposing it as well as the surrounding muscles and tendons. Olga tried to stifle her cries, but the pain was so excruciating she continued whimpering for several minutes. Still, Olga felt relieved, knowing she would be safe. Years later, she would tell her own children how she felt after her ordeal: "I knew when I saw my leg I was not going to be taken by the guerrillas. I even thought I might never walk again. But it was worth it, because I wanted to live. I didn't want to be taken from my mother and my family. I also wanted to have my own family someday."

The next day, when the conscription officers showed up to take Olga away, they were shown the young woman's injury. With skeptical eyes, they scrutinized Olga and asked what happened. When Eleni explained Olga had hurt herself in a kitchen accident, the officers grunted angrily and stormed off.

The next few weeks were difficult for Olga, but eventually her injury healed and she regained full use of her leg. One of her sisters had been taken by the guerrillas in her place, but she was younger and less mature. After a few weeks of service, Olga's sister proved so inept as a guerrilla fighter, her commanders let her go.

Now that the family was together again, their goal was to survive their virtual imprisonment. They had enough to eat thanks to the efforts of Eleni, although she put her life at risk many times by holding back some of the crops she had harvested for the guerrillas. The family members also kept their distance from the Communist leaders, making sure not to offend them in any way and doing whatever was asked of them.

By early 1948, the war was not going well for the Communists, and they were losing ground to the Greek government forces. The national army had made so much progress that they were only a mile from Olga's village, encamped in a nearby mountain known as the Great Ridge. In February of that year, the government launched a massive assault against the Communist forces in the area, hoping to crush their resistance and win back all the territory the Communists had gained. When the battle was over, however, the Communist fighters repelled the Greek army and sent them scurrying back up the Great Ridge. Olga and her family would continue to be captives in their village and could only dream of freedom.

Several weeks after the government defeat, even worse news hit Olga's family. Since the war was going so badly for the Communists, they decided to relocate all children from occupied areas to nearby Communist countries. This meant all children would be taken from their mothers.

Eleni panicked when she heard the news. Her children would be taken from her, and they would be sent to faraway places, perhaps never to be reunited again. It was inconceivable. She had to act quickly to combat the forces that were working to tear her family apart.

Very soon she had her answer: Her children would have to escape from the village and seek refuge with the government forces encamped on the Great Ridge. There was only one problem. Another one of Eleni's daughters, Lillia, had been taken by the guerrillas to work the fields, and she was now with them somewhere in the mountains. What would happen to her if the rest of the children escaped?

Eleni agonized over what to do, knowing that time was running short. Already there were rumors that the gathering of children would start any day, which meant her children might be taken from her within the week. She would have to act fast.

The following evening, Eleni gathered her four remaining children and told them of her plan. Olga, age nineteen, would be responsible for leading three of her siblings to freedom while Eleni stayed behind to watch out for Lillia. Eleni told Olga it was her responsibility to care for her siblings, and Olga accepted the task. She felt overwhelmed by the responsibility but understood she had no choice. The escape would take place the next night.

After tearful goodbyes and a promise by Eleni that she would meet up with her children as soon as she and her other daughter could arrange their own escape, Olga and her siblings began their dangerous march toward freedom. Although the Great Ridge was only a mile away, the escape route would take them through a vast wheat field littered with landmines and marked by a number of enemy guardhouses placed strategically along the perimeter. But first they had to meet up with another group of refugees in the lower village who had asked to join in the escape.

When Olga met up with them, she was shocked to find sixteen people in the party; she thought the group would include only her uncle, his wife, and their two children. "I thought there was no way twenty of us would get past all the guards and landmines," Olga recounted. "But my mother told me we had to go, so that is what we did. Inside, though, I thought we were all going to die. I only hoped I could save my sisters and brother."

As they wended their way through the wheat field, the line of refugees began to thin out. In a short while, Olga found herself and two other women separated from the rest of the group. She didn't know how it had happened, but they were alone. She tried calling out for the others, but her calls went unanswered.

Realizing they could not stay where they were, the three stragglers began walking in the same general direction as when they started their march, and after a few minutes, they ran into the rest of the group, who had doubled back to find them. Olga hugged her sisters and brother and thanked the heavens that everyone was still safe.

At about this time, several hundred yards away, a guerrilla search party was combing the wheat field looking for possible defectors. The local guerrilla leader ordered his men to apprehend or kill any escapees they found.

Olga and the other nineteen refugees continued their harrowing journey toward the Great Ridge, and in the early-morning hours, they reached the base of the mountain. Freedom was close. All they had to do was climb to the top and be rescued. But they had to wait until morning so the government soldiers would not mistake them for spies.

At the first light of dawn, Olga called out to the soldiers above to allow the refugees to climb up. At first there was no answer, but after a few moments a voice responded: "Come on up, but in single file. Follow the path and you'll see an opening in the wire."

The group followed the soldier's instructions, twenty desperate individuals snaking their way up the mountain toward their salvation. A few hundred yards away, a guerrilla guard who had spent the entire night looking for the refugees observed the scene and shook his head in amazement, shocked that they had gotten away from him. He didn't shoot at them for fear of giving away his position. The twenty refugees had won their freedom.

Olga and her siblings were eventually sent to a refugee camp in a coastal city of western Greece, where they anxiously awaited news about their mother. But days and then weeks passed with no information. Then, in late September 1948, their grandfather arrived at the camp with something he needed to tell them. It was that day that Olga's world came crashing down around her, for that was the day she learned of her mother's awful fate.

When the Communist leaders discovered that Olga and her siblings had escaped, they imprisoned Eleni and tortured her for her treasonous acts. Her crime: allowing her children to flee the village. Her punishment: death by firing squad. On August 28, 1948, that sentence had been carried out.

After learning of her mother's execution, Olga went into a deep depression. "I didn't want to live anymore," she admitted. "With my mother gone, I had no reason to live. But then I remembered what she told me about my sisters and brother, and I knew I had to keep going. I made a promise to her and I had to keep it."

The ensuing months were a blur to Olga. Then, in March 1949, she and her siblings learned they were going to be moved to the United States, where they would be reunited with their father. Olga's fourth sibling, Lillia, was still being held by the Communists, and the family had heard no news about her. They could only hope for the best.

The trip across the ocean on the USNS Marine Carp, a converted warship, was torture for Olga. She remained in bed in her steerage compartment for almost the entire two-week journey, eating very little and becoming dehydrated due to excess vomiting. When the ship finally pulled into New York harbor, Olga had to be helped off by her siblings.

After the Gatzoyiannis children cleared customs, Olga's father loaded them into his leased car and drove them to Worcester, Massachusetts, where they would start a new life together. The reunion between father and children was strained, but for Olga it was a relief to have him there so she would no longer have to shoulder the burden of the family's survival. "I thanked God we now had a father to take care of us," she said. "I could barely take care of myself at that point, let alone two sisters and a brother."

Olga was miserable in her new environment; Worcester was an old factory city with rows and rows of tenement houses. Her family lived in such a house, on the first floor, in a poorer part of the city. Her father worked as a chef at a restaurant, earning barely enough to pay the bills. Olga lamented her station in life: She lived in a place she hated, she couldn't speak the language, her mother had been brutally killed the previous year, and there were no prospects that the family's fortunes would ever change—they were destined to be poor forever.

As bad as things were for Olga, they were about to get much worse. A few weeks after her arrival in America, her father took her to a doctor because she had a lump of some kind on her neck. After taking one look at the growth, the doctor ordered Olga to be taken to a hospital immediately so he could operate on her. The growth might be cancer. Olga was terrified about what lay in front of her, but in a way, she hoped her disease would take her life. If it did, she thought, at least her misery would end.

When the surgery was over and Olga was strong enough to get out of the hospital bed, she walked over to the mirror to see herself. She knew the doctor had removed something on her neck, but she didn't know exactly how bad the surgery was. None of her family had told her what her neck looked like. When she finally observed the condition of her neck in the mirror, she almost fainted. A good portion of it had been removed—she was horribly disfigured. Olga buried her face in her hands and cried. As bad as her life had been before, it had just gotten much, much worse.

For the next few weeks, Olga suffered through depression, rarely leaving the house or seeking out company. Life simply had no meaning for her. "I just wanted to die," she remembered many years later. "My mother was gone, I never went out, I couldn't work, and because of my neck I was sure I would never marry and have children. What kind of life would I have with no children?"

But soon, Olga and her family received some wonderful news. Olga's sister Lillia, the one who had been taken by the Communists, had escaped captivity and was headed to America. She would be reunited with the family any day. When she arrived in Worcester two days later, there was a raucous celebration in which even Olga participated. For a while, at least, Olga's spirits lifted.

Olga was about to get some more good news. Several months later, her father had received a letter from a young man named Dino who grew up near Olga's village, asking his permission to marry Olga. Dino had never actually met Olga, but he knew she had a spotless reputation and he would be honored to be her husband. Olga's father agreed to the match.

Olga was excited about the news, but she was also uncertain if the marriage would ever take place. She didn't know if her suitor would be up to it, given her appearance. "Will he still want to marry me when he sees my neck?" Olga wondered. "Or will he be too ashamed to be with me because of the way I look?"

In September 1951, Olga and her father greeted Dino when he arrived at New York harbor. Dino beamed with excitement as he hugged his future father-in-law and kissed his future wife's hand. And much to Olga's joy, later that day when she showed Dino the terrible scar on her neck, he simply dismissed it as a minor imperfection. "I remember what he said to me when he saw my neck," Olga recounted. "'We all have something wrong with us. That's nothing to worry about.' Right then, I knew my life was going to get better. That's when I thought to myself that all my sacrifices were worth it."

Dino and Olga married in October 1951 and in just a few short years had four children. During that time, two of Olga's younger sisters married as well. The three families eventually moved into a tenement home in which each family occupied one floor.

For Olga, those early married years in Worcester were some of the best of her life. She had four beautiful children and two sisters living in the same home, and soon her sisters had children of their own. Life was wonderful. That the family was poor was not a problem for Olga, because all she cared about at the time was her children.

One day, however, Olga went to a toy store to buy a small gift for a friend's baby, taking along one of her young sons. With only twenty-five cents in her pocket, she couldn't afford much, but it was enough for what she intended to buy. But when they entered the toy store, Olga's son saw a race car set he liked, and he excitedly asked his mother if he could buy it. Olga said no, but the boy persisted. She said no again, but the boy wouldn't stop. Finally, Olga shouted at her son in Greek and then smacked him in the rear end. The boy looked down in disappointment and followed his mother down the aisle to the ten-cent toys.

Later in life, Olga would recount that day with tears in her eyes: "My son only wanted a little toy, and I couldn't give it to him. I felt so worthless. That's the day I decided we needed to do something. I didn't know how, but I promised myself we would not be poor forever."

Olga's opportunity came two years later by pure happenstance. The family was returning from a day at the beach when one of Olga's sons had to use the bathroom. Olga told her husband to take the next exit so they could pull over somewhere. As Dino drove off the exit ramp, they entered the small, affluent town of Needham, Massachusetts. Olga marveled at the beautiful homes that lined the street, all with lush yards. When they reached the downtown area, Olga spotted a vacant storefront that had a "FOR RENT" sign on the front window. She wrote down the number on a piece of paper and placed it in her purse.

The next day, she mentioned the vacant store to Dino and suggested they could open a small restaurant at the site. At first Dino showed no interest, but Olga was insistent, and soon Dino was on the phone with the landlord. That one call would change the family's fortunes forever.

Within two months, Dino and Olga opened a pizza restaurant at the vacant store. And then, only two years after that, the restaurant had done so well the couple bought a three-bedroom house in Needham, which came with an in-ground swimming pool. Olga had realized the American dream, but more importantly, she had fulfilled the promise she made to herself years earlier after her visit to the toy store.

On a daily basis, Olga would get her children ready for school and work at the pizza place for the noon rush. Then, she would pick the children up from school and go back to work for the evening rush. Olga worked fourteen hours a day, seven days a week, doing various jobs, but she couldn't have been happier. Her family was thriving. "I would do anything for my children," she would say, "even if I had to kill myself working. I always remembered what my mother did for me, and I wanted to do the same for my children."

But Olga had her down moments as well. The death of her mother continued to haunt her, and she was prone to anxiety attacks. Her doctors explained that these attacks were brought on by the horrors she had experienced when she was younger, and all they could do was give her anti-anxiety medication. With the medication, however, Olga learned to cope.

There were also setbacks with the pizza business. Three times, a local competitor who was connected with the Mafia hired arsonists to burn down Olga and Dino's pizza place, but three times Olga and Dino built the business back up. "I was not going to let anybody stop me," Olga said about the fires, "not even the Mafia. The FBI told them to stop burning down my business, and for some reason, they obeyed."

After the third fire, Dino and Olga were forced to buy the block of stores the pizza place was situated on, because their landlord refused to rent to them anymore. This proved to be a blessing in disguise, as Olga's eyes were opened to the world of real estate. Soon, Olga and Dino opened eight additional pizza restaurants in nearby towns, working them all themselves or with their children and other relatives. Eventually Olga and Dino bought more commercial property, quickly becoming real estate magnates. It seemed as though everything Olga touched turned to gold; her restaurants were thriving and her commercial real estate was bringing in substantial rental income. There was no stopping Olga. The poor immigrant who couldn't afford a toy for her son just a few short years prior was now a successful businesswoman, earning enough money to give her children a very comfortable life. All she asked of them in return was to study hard and do well in school.

Olga's children did not disappoint her. Two attended Harvard University, one attended Tufts University, and the last went to Boston College. Two would go on to become doctors, the other two lawyers. Olga would proudly announce to anyone willing to listen, "I might be an uneducated village peasant, but this stupid woman produced four smart children—two doctors and two lawyers. Not too bad."

Olga and Dino retired from work in 1981 and spent the next twenty-five years enjoying life, traveling all over the United States and Europe, and spending time with their children and grandchildren. Dino died in 2006, and Olga's own health began to deteriorate after that, but the two enjoyed many good years together as husband and wife.

When she passed away, Olga still lived in the same home in Needham that she'd bought with her husband in 1966.

Olga Gatzoyiannis is an inspiration to any woman who must overcome oppression, tragedy, hopelessness, and poverty to achieve success. She found what motivated her the most and used it to fuel her determined spirit. In Olga's words, "If a poor, uneducated shepherd girl like me can make it, anyone can. All it takes is hard work and sacrifice, and the willingness to take a chance. But the greatest motivation is love of family. You don't work hard for yourself; you do it for your children."

If you'd like to make a donation in Olga's name, please visit Beth Israel Deaconess Hospital Needham at https://www.bidneedham.org/.

Lynn

So often we wonder how one simple action might have altered the course of our lives. What if we'd done *that* instead of *this*? What if we'd stood *there* instead of *here*? What if a line had been shorter, a server had brought the bill sooner...

What if?

Of course, we can't go back in time. We have to live the life that is presented to us as best we can, realizing there might come moments that change our destinies. Such has been the case for Lynn Julian Crisci—a survivor of the 2013 Boston Marathon bombings.

In 2006, Lynn was a musician who had written close to one hundred songs, found airtime on university airwaves, and had her music featured on more than thirty compilation CDs internationally. *Rolling Stone* magazine dubbed her "Nashville's Version of Fiona Apple." Lynn lived and breathed music, and it looked as if she had a bright future in the industry.

That future was cut short by a single misstep on stage during a club show in Brighton, Massachusetts. Lynn slipped on cords that were not taped down and unknowingly began a medical odyssey that took years to resolve or even improve. Lynn suffered from debilitating vertigo that forced her into a wheelchair, which in turn led to deteriorating hand-eye coordination and overall weakness. Perhaps worst of all, her doctors labeled her "depressed" and could find no medical reason for her symptoms. But Lynn did not give up. She searched for a doctor who would take her situation seriously, and nearly a year after her accident, the truth was revealed: Lynn had suffered neck damage and traumatic brain injury (TBI) during her fall.

Lynn felt vindicated; she was finally pointed in the proper direction to find help.

Determined to regain her independence, Lynn found homecare to help her with simple tasks such as bathing, and she enlisted in speech therapy while she healed. In 2008, once she could move about, Lynn enrolled in cognitive, balance, and physical therapies, which were designed to help her deal with her mental and physical limitations. By 2009, Lynn was no longer bed-bound or restricted to a wheelchair. By the summer of 2012, she began to walk alone, without the use of a cane, for the first time since her accident.

Also in 2012, Lynn learned some news that brought more clarity to her brain injury. Surprisingly, it was her dermatologist who mentioned the words Ehlers-Danlos syndrome after hearing about Lynn's stretched-out neck ligament, which had never healed from the stage accident. Ehlers-Danlos syndrome (EDS) is a connective tissue disorder in which the collagen in the body is essentially broken and the joints are hypermobile, meaning they all painfully over-rotate. When a tendon or ligament stretches out mildly with repetition, or severely just one time, it doesn't have the elasticity needed to return to its original shape. That is what had happened to Lynn's neck.

By 2013, seven years after the accident, Lynn was reclaiming her life. She had resolved many of her previously unanswered medical questions, had found the resources she needed to heal, and was walking without assistance. Though her life was normalizing, Lynn no longer could perform as a musician. Brain injuries change people. Lynn used to sing, write original songs, and play guitar every day. But after the accident, simply raising her voice created a pressure in her head that was too painful to manage. Lynn never returned to music but instead began an acting career and booked regional film work. One freak accident on stage altered the course of Lynn's life; however, she was learning to adapt by starting a new career.

"In the beginning of 2013, I was *so* proud of myself," Lynn says, "for fighting through my physical pain and getting out of that wheelchair; for relearning to walk normally again; for advocating for my own mental health until I found a doctor that finally diagnosed my first TBI; for mourning the loss of my music career and moving forward; for finding the courage to take acting classes and enrolling in the theatre arts program of UMass Boston; and for acting in a dozen regional film projects. I *finally* found hope again and truly believed 2013 was the beginning of my new career as a professional actress."

On April 15, 2013, Lynn continued a longstanding tradition of many Boston residents. She, along with much of the city, prepared for the running of the annual Boston Marathon, which ended a block and a half from her apartment. In past years, Lynn and her partner, Doug, had joined the crowds standing on Boylston Street to watch the runners cross the finish line. Typically, they would arrive early enough to watch the fastest racers finish and would stand near Exeter Street, which was about a block before the actual finish line, where they could watch the action on the nearby Jumbotron.

This year, however, they decided to try something a little different. Lynn walked down Boylston with her service dog, looking for an open table where they could sit and see the Jumbotron. She nabbed a spot only two storefronts down from where she normally stood. It was a typical race day. The street was buzzing with excitement as a steady stream of runners ended their 26.2-mile trek from Hopkinton. There was no reason to believe that this Marathon Monday would end any differently than the previous ones.

As late morning turned into early afternoon, Lynn and Doug decided to head home. But they were delayed for several reasons: two girls on their cell phones in the restroom, a long search for a trash can to throw away a red lollipop that fell from Lynn's pocket, and a restaurant server too overwhelmed to bring the check. Lynn and Doug were still waiting for the check when the unimaginable happened:

an explosion. The blast, which happened near the finish line, was much more massive than what appeared on television screens. Within five seconds, smoke and debris shrouded an entire five-story building. The sidewalk shook, bouncing the metal chairs on which Lynn and Doug sat. No one around Lynn moved; no one panicked. No one seemed to understand what had just happened. Lynn began to worry. Doug tried to calm her down, saying it was probably just a transformer that blew. About a year before, one had blown on the same street and caused a huge fire. Very quickly, others around them began muttering the same thing until ten seconds later when a second explosion occurred.

Lynn's dog, Lil Stinker, jumped up from her lap and began scratching Lynn's face in a panic. This snapped Lynn into action; she was the first person to jump up from her chair. To keep her little dog from running away in fear, Lynn wrapped her arms tightly around him and held him against her chest. The scene around her looked like a still photo with everyone frozen in fear after the second bomb exploded, yet Lynn felt forced to flee because of her dog's reaction. For all she knew, a third bomb could detonate at any second.

As people began to comprehend the severity of the situation on Boylston Street, chaos and fear unfolded. Lynn had nowhere to run.

"In front of me was a wooden wall separating the spectators from the media," she recalls. "To the left was a single-file corridor that maneuvered spectators around the finish line.

To the right was where both of the bombs had just exploded in the last ten seconds. I don't remember thinking any of that consciously, though. I simply pointed behind me to the entrance to the bar we had been dining at. It was only after I reached the back of the bar that I consciously thought about how we could get to safety from there. Having worked in the restaurant business for fifteen years, I knew that by law every bar would have a back exit door in case of a fire. I was determined to find it in order to escape. I choked on the stench of sulfur, fighting to breathe, straining to see through my tears, hoping to hear Doug over the panicked cries of strangers, and watching people wander back toward the sidewalk."

Lynn tried to run into the bar, but the entrance was blocked by curious, intoxicated people. They stood frozen in place, too confused about what had just happened outside to move. Lynn repeatedly barked a simple order at them: "Move, move, move, move!" Finally, whether from fear or realization, they did. Still, none of them understood the tragedy that had just transpired. Those who had heard the noise and seen the commotion outside thought they had missed something exciting and attempted to shove their way out the door past Lynn. Meanwhile, the people who had been on the street and witnessed the explosions tried to push their way past Lynn *into* the bar to get to safety. The bar itself was very narrow, with stools on both sides of the walkway. Chaos ensued as people pushed in every direction, and Lynn felt herself getting squeezed by the crush of the crowd. She had no way to shield her body, because her arms were still tightly wrapped around her chest to protect her small dog. (She later discovered this resulted in both her shoulders partially dislocating. Due to her connective tissue disorder, both of her shoulders now painfully pop out a bit every time she lies down.)

Lynn continued to fight through the crowd until finally she found a door in the rear of the building. She ordered anyone who would listen to go out that door. Some people jumped at the chance for safety and left immediately. Others refused, saying they wanted to go out to take pictures. Lynn, Doug, and the group of people who had decided to follow them exited through the back door to find a stairwell that spilled out onto Newbury Street, which paralleled Boylston. Even though they were one street over, Lynn was still choking on sulfur from the explosions. She was certain the blasts had to have been intentional.

Lynn passed swarms of people headed to Boylston Street to see what had caused the explosions, thinking they were celebratory gestures of some kind. She hysterically tried to warn them about the explosions, but once again people's fascination with the unknown led them to believe they'd missed something like a fireworks display. They continued to shove past her toward the marathon route, and Lynn proceeded to her apartment, pushing against the sea of people.

By the time Lynn finally arrived at home, she was in shock and a complete state of panic. She was crying and hyperventilating, and she looked disheveled. She pleaded with the concierge of her building to lock the doors and not let anyone else leave the building. At that point, she still feared more bombs would detonate. The concierge just chuckled at Lynn's odd request and assumed she'd had a little too much to drink, a common occurrence in Boston on Marathon Monday. News of the explosions had not yet spread, and the concierge had no reason to believe Lynn.

Lynn sought comfort in a friend's apartment, where she could be with other people. As soon as she sat down, though, searing pain alerted her that her lower back was injured. Lynn had been fueled by adrenaline that afternoon, and her only concern had been getting to safety. Now that she was out of harm's way, her ailments came into focus. Not only did she find that her shoulders had separated, she also recognized some familiar symptoms: the room spun, her ears rung, she felt like vomiting and passing out, and everything sounded as if she were underwater. She felt as if she had traveled back to 2006, to the night of her stage accident.

Though Lynn knew she had suffered some kind of injury, she did not immediately head to the emergency room. Having learned more about the explosions after watching them continuously replayed on the news, Lynn understood that the hospitals would be inundated with people with severe wounds. She decided to wait until the following day before seeking medical treatment, and even then, she called to ask permission prior to heading to the hospital.

When Lynn was admitted to the ER, the staff held her there all day for observation but performed no testing or treatment. Lynn repeatedly was offered only one thing: a priest for counseling. Just as in 2006, the doctors and nurses believed Lynn had psychological trauma instead of a physical injury because no one could find the root of her symptoms. Lynn asked to see her neurologist, who also worked at that hospital, but the ER staff refused. Because she was not being treated for anything, Lynn requested to be discharged. On her paperwork, she noticed that the doctor noted the reason for Lynn's visit was only "anxiety," not even mentioning she was a survivor of the Boston Marathon bombings. When she saw the discharge nurse, Lynn very uncharacteristically shook the paperwork at her and cried, "You know, a bomb just blew up in front of me. This is not okay!" Angry that once again no one believed she had a real injury, Lynn wobbled out of the hospital, unable to steady herself. She spent the next days alternating between crying and yelling. Her world had been flipped upside down again, and no one cared to understand it because her issues were not visible. Lynn was frustrated and confused.

"I don't know why it was so ridiculously difficult for me to convince my doctors that I had suffered a second brain injury," she says. "It could have been any number of things: simple ignorance, hospital agenda, or doctors thinking I was seeking something more like attention or money.

"I was not aware of this after my stage accident, but suffering even one minor concussion greatly increases your risk of suffering another one. This is especially true in the two months following your brain injury. That is the window of opportunity for treatment and lifestyle changes that can result in healing your brain tissue the most: low lights only; low sounds only; very little reading, if any; very little phone and computer time, if any; lots of rest; extra sleep; large doses of Omega 3 and other supplements daily; etc. I was at even greater risk for traumatic brain injury because of my connective tissue disorder, which left my brain tissue weaker.

"Because I did not know all that in 2006, I missed that window of recovery, and I probably further damaged my brain with bright lights and loud sounds. Because my doctors did not know all that in 2013, I missed that window of recovery and I probably further damaged my brain— *again*. The doctors had me convinced that my post-traumatic stress disorder was clouding my perspective of the world, exaggerating my symptoms. They had me convinced that I did not have a second brain injury."

Over time, Lynn's symptoms diminished. It took months before her vertigo disappeared, and the persistent ringing in her ears was still steady but no longer extremely loud. She still suffered from a myriad of disabling symptoms: daily pressure headaches; weekly migraines; chronic brain fog and short-term memory loss; severe lower back, leg, and shoulder pain; hearing loss; hyperacusis (increased sound sensitivity and low tolerance to usual environmental sounds); extreme sensitivity to light and odors; and constant hypervigilance along with a debilitating fear of going outside alone. She was healing slowly but would never be completely cured. She knew that. Whether or not her undiagnosed internal injuries ever disappeared, she also now found herself struggling with PTSD caused by the explosions she witnessed.

"What I actually saw has blurred together over the years," Lynn says. "The first bomb exploded over five stories high in as many seconds. People were attacked by the device and then swallowed whole as they disappeared in the tsunami of smoke. As soon as I got to my friend's apartment, he kept the local Boston news on all day, which featured graphic coverage of the bomb exploding, over and over and over. This felt like it went on for months—until I was hearing the bomb go off in my sleep. It would wake me up around 2:49 every morning; the first explosion had gone off at 2:49 p.m. The Internet and social media were full of graphic photos of the survivors with the most severe external injuries. Each bloody moment captured on film became burned in my brain, where it remains to this day."

Lynn joined a support group for injured survivors of the bombings. She came to realize that she was not the only person who viewed the world differently after the incident. Many of the survivors wanted to stay safely indoors and became hypervigilant of their surroundings. They no longer thought of the world as a safe place where nothing bad would happen to them. Instead, they knew something bad would happen again; they just didn't know when.

In November 2013, Lynn was at one of her weekly support group meetings when the announcement came that the Boston Athletic Association, which organizes the Boston Marathon, would allow survivors of the bombings to run in the 2014 race. The room erupted with cheers and applause. The survivors were thrilled at the chance to have a way to mentally overcome the attack that had disrupted their lives.

Lynn quietly slipped out to cry in the bathroom as the rest of the room carried on with its celebration. Lynn felt defeated. Many of the survivors had visible external injuries. They were the ones receiving ample support, ranging from doctors and specialists to friends, family, and even strangers. People with invisible injuries, like Lynn's, were still trying to be diagnosed more than six months later. The fact that no one believed her for a second time took a toll on her confidence and self-esteem.

Due to her many undiagnosed injuries, Lynn didn't think she could even walk the Boston Marathon. Her previous brain injury, coupled with her injuries from the explosion, caused her to walk strangely, as if she were intoxicated. She did not want to cover that race course looking like a drunkard. Additionally, her PTSD would not allow her to even imagine walking the race route all by herself. To Lynn, the once-confident city girl who attended every outdoor concert and celebration in Boston, any large gathering now seemed an unsafe target for terrorist attacks.

"If I could change one thing, it would be to help everyone

understand traumatic brain injury, especially my survivor peers," Lynn says. "TBI, even when it's an entirely internal injury, is as disabling as an external injury and deserves the same emotional support from the peer community and physical treatments from the medical community to heal."

By the time Lynn went back to the next survivor meeting, she had convinced herself that finishing the Boston Marathon would give her much-needed, priceless self-confidence. She had never run for pleasure in her life, let alone run an official race, but she told herself, "Who cares what other people think about me? I'm going to do this!" And she began training that November. Because of her neurological condition, Lynn started walking on a treadmill. For the first month, she held on to the sides of the machine because of her balance issues. Slowly, she learned how to walk without holding on to the sides and picked up her pace. By the second month, Lynn incorporated very slow jogging into her training and also began running without holding on to the sides of the treadmill. To Lynn's great joy, she was beginning to overcome some of her fears about her physical limitations. More importantly, she was beginning to regain her confidence.

In January 2014, Lynn had a major breakthrough. She discovered a CNN video on YouTube in which the Boston bombings were reenacted. This video, which was shot in a desert, showed where the shrapnel landed and the trajectory of the sound waves. Scientists mapped the sound waves and found that they went on for miles. The blast was low to the ground, so many people received injuries to their lower extremities. Lynn was the closest person to the bomb who was seated, not standing. The explosions affected her torso because she was sitting down. Everything was fitting together like a puzzle. The blasts caused the sidewalk to shake violently. Because Lynn had a connective tissue disorder and was seated on a metal chair without cushions, her body reverberated more than it otherwise would have. The metal chair just kept shaking underneath her so that it herniated some of the discs in her spine. Her body lacked the protective collagen it needed to prevent that. This type of injury probably would not have happened to someone without a connective tissue disorder.

Up to that point, Lynn had never heard of blast force trauma, a TBI typically occurring in soldiers with exposure to detonated bombs. Because blast force trauma usually affects only military personnel, few doctors outside the armed forces have any knowledge of the symptoms or diagnosis. This was the reason Lynn had such difficulty convincing medical professionals that her symptoms were real. But in fact, Lynn was more susceptible to brain trauma because of two things: her prior brain injury and her Ehlers-Danlos Syndrome. The lack of protective collagen in her head allowed her brain to shake around like a gelatin mold during the explosions, causing extensive damage.

With the newly acquired knowledge of blast force trauma,

Lynn finally had what she so desperately needed: the reason for her symptoms—brain injury—and the evidence of how it occurred. Lynn showed the video to her neurologist, who was finally able to medically validate her internal injuries. This allowed Lynn to receive the support she knew she needed. She was approved for vestibular therapy (for balance), acupuncture (for pain), physical therapy and myofascial release therapy (for her back), speech therapy and occupational therapy (for her brain injury), cognitive behavioral therapy and psychological therapy (for her PTSD), and more.

This validation also gave her the courage and confidence to continue training for the 2014 Boston Marathon. She moved her runs outside, where she no longer had anything to hold on to. She ran every day, weathering the rain, ice, and snow. She would get lost on her longer training runs because her brain injury caused chronic short-term memory loss. Though that once would have upset her, she now laughed it off as a minor issue. Because of her EDS, Lynn suffered from micro-tears in certain connective joints, such as hips and ankles. Instead of quitting, she followed the advice of an experienced marathoner and mentor, Jack Fultz, who told her to change her gait every mile to prevent injury. Lynn had so many reasons to quit, but instead she dug deep to find the strength and confidence to persevere. She persisted.

On April 21, 2014, Lynn found herself at the starting line of the Boston Marathon, lining up with the other mobility-impaired runners. Prior to starting, she had been thinking about her survivor family, the victims, and the entire ordeal from the previous year. When it was time for the race to begin, Lynn thought, "I can't do this! I've been crying for the last three hours!" Sarah Reinertsen, a professional marathoner who was also running in the mobility-impaired division, came to the rescue. A complete stranger, Sarah stood with Lynn while she cried for the hour before the race and helped her find the courage to start her 26.2-mile healing journey.

Along the way, Lynn had moments of panic and terror, especially when she was alone on the course. Being a mobility-impaired runner meant she started the race even before the professional athletes to allow her more time on the course. Because of this, she was not always surrounded by other runners. Whenever she heard a loud nose, such as a race truck zooming by her or a helicopter overhead, her PTSD would cause Lynn to drop to the ground in fear and begin crying. But each time this happened, she would rise up and remind herself that she'd vowed to finish this race no matter what.

Lynn had committed to the race, and she meant it. By mile twenty-three, Lynn was struggling. She was dragging her leg behind her because she had so many micro-tears in her hip. The medics tried to coax her to come to the tent so they could massage her injury, but she refused. Lynn thought, "I don't care what people think of me. Let them look at me and laugh at the funny way I'm walking. I'll laugh with them. But I am not going to let that stop me from completing this race."

It was at this point that her "angel," Sarah Reinertsen, reappeared from out of nowhere, smiling and assuring Lynn that they could make it the last three miles to the finish line together. Lynn was convinced she was going to finish, but she had no idea how hard it would be. The last half-mile of the race course forced Lynn to walk past both bombing sites and through a hundred thousand screaming spectators.

She stopped cold at the entrance to Boylston Street, asking Sarah, "Everyone's screaming. Why are they screaming? Make them stop!"

Assuming she was joking, Sarah simply laughed, saying, "They're not screaming. They're cheering!"

Lynn was sent into a severe panic attack and could not be convinced she was safe. "I can't finish. Just let me go home! I live right over there," she begged Sarah as she pointed to her apartment building.

Sarah, now realizing that Lynn was serious, explained that the only way to "go home" was to cross the finish line first. Due to the high security on Boylston Street, this was true. So, that is how Lynn found the courage to face her biggest fear: being at the bombing sites themselves. She had to cross the finish line in order to get home.

And she did.

Crossing the finish line of the marathon restored a lot of the confidence that had been stripped away from her over the years. She had been a successful musician before the stage accident and a budding actress before the marathon bombing. Her self-esteem had been wrapped up in the public personas she'd once created. But when those personas disappeared and she no longer could sing or act, she didn't know what to make of herself; she didn't know who she was. Completing the marathon allowed her to believe in herself again.

To this day, Lynn's body is still healing. She deals with permanent hearing loss, uses hearing aids, and experiences chronic pain, daily headaches, and disabling weekly migraines. Her immune system has become weak and she has developed severe allergies and multiple chemical sensitivity (MCS) to her surroundings: barometric pressure changes due to rain and snow and smells such as freshly cut grass, flowers, perfumes, cigarettes, cleaners, gasoline, and paint. She never had these allergies or MCS before suffering the blast force trauma brain injury and inhaling clouds of sulfur dust and sidewalk debris. Now she has to carry a surgical mask with her at all times in the event she comes into contact with a pungent scent that might activate a migraine. She visits her maintenance doctors and therapists three to five times a week.

One thing that frustrates Lynn is that family and friends think she should be recovered by now. Most days, she looks healthy on the outside, and she puts on a brave face for the world, but she's far from fully healed. She will never be completely rehabilitated to her old self.

"Five years later, I *still* cannot tell my survivor story without reliving it," Lynn explains. "One of my goals is to get to the point where I can tell my story without getting triggered by it and breaking down. Through a priceless charity organization, Strength to Strength (STS), I have found the support I so desperately craved. Strength to Strength unites survivors and victims' families from terrorist attacks internationally. STS members showed me that time *does* help heal and that I *will* be able to share my story, someday, without reliving it."

Lynn understands that her life is a constant series of daily choices and that her decisions will affect her health. She auditions for small acting roles, ones that require her to be under bright lights for a few days at a time. She knows the lighting might cause a migraine. Choosing to commit to those days of filming is also choosing to be out of commission for the rest of the week afterward. If she does anything physical, such as dancing for several hours at a wedding, she understands that her EDS will cause micro-tears throughout her body and she'll be in pain. She lives each day knowing that even the smallest decision she makes can have a serious impact on her brain or body.

Lynn uses her experiences as a platform for change, with the goal of helping others with similar problems. She did not have the level of support she needed during either of her brain injury journeys. She volunteers as a patient advocate with multiple organizations to create awareness about concussion and TBI symptoms and treatments. Her goal is to prevent other people from suffering needlessly the way she did.

She also speaks at medical conferences to educate doctors. She feels that when doctors have discussions about brain injuries, it is always better to have someone present who can speak from first-person experience. Lynn works with pharmaceutical companies on better treatments and she talks with patients so they don't make same mistakes she did.

Lynn supports clinical trials and volunteers for medical studies whenever she can. She learned about a trial for hyperbaric oxygen therapy (HBOT), an approved therapy for limb loss that is currently being tested on brain injuries. Both her brain injury specialist in Boston and her neurologist informed her that a brain injury does not heal any further after one and a half to two years. They said there was no longer a need for Lynn to have any more follow-up visits. Lynn convinced them to examine her one final time after she completed a two-month HBOT clinical trial in New Orleans. They agreed. When Lynn returned to each of their offices after the trial, the doctors were shocked at her improvement. In the neuro-psych tests administered throughout the medical study, she performed noticeably better than she had before the forty HBOT treatments. Her PTSD was also about half its previous level. Whereas before the HBOT treatment Lynn would never leave the house alone, after the HBOT treatment, she was able to do so with much less debilitating fear. Lynn has her independence back. Her brain tissues also have healed significantly, and she is able to speak and walk normally most of the time. Lynn proved to her doctors that this new therapy does help heal brain injury and PTSD. Perhaps her results also influenced the major Boston hospital network for which her doctors worked, as it is now conducting its own clinical trial on the effects of HBOT and brain injuries. Thanks to Lynn's persistence, change is happening.

Lynn is doing everything she can to help people in situations similar to hers. She became a Massachusetts ambassador for the U.S. Pain Foundation. She volunteered on the advisory panel for the One Fund Boston, a charity organized to offer financial support to the marathon bombing survivors. She fought for inclusion of bombing survivors who suffered internal injuries, such as hearing loss, brain injury, and PTSD, since most of the One Fund's $120 million donations went to people with external injuries. Lynn also volunteered on the advisory panel of the Massachusetts Resiliency Center, which offered support and resources to those affected by the marathon bombing until closing in summer 2017.

Being a patient advocate and survivor ambassador for worthy causes gives Lynn a greater sense of purpose. She has regained her self-esteem by being able to offer help and guidance to those whose injuries are similar to her own. Lynn Julian Crisci turned the worst chain of events into a remarkable tale of courage and spirit. She does not plan to stop any time soon.

"I find great satisfaction in being a volunteer patient advocate for several organizations. So, I'm happy to create awareness by educating anyone who asks about brain injury," Lynn says. "Sometimes, when my symptoms are flaring up, every day feels like a marathon. I break down into doable chunks what seem to others like small tasks. I count down the hours and the tasks until I don't have anything left to give. Having permanent chronic injuries forces you to make choices about what is most important to you, all day, every day. On the bright side, you learn to live very much in the moment and appreciate the little pleasures of life so much more."

In addition to raising awareness about PTSD and TBI, Lynn wants her message to be one of hope: "I fought my way out of that wheelchair and across that finish line. If I can do it, so can you!"

And to this day, Lynn carries a red lollipop in her pocket or purse—just as she did on April 15, 2013—to remind herself to be patient and that everything happens for a reason.

....

If you'd like to support an organization close to Lynn's heart, please visit Strength to Strength at stosglobal.org.

Rasheera

Gazing up at the ceiling from the moving hospital bed, Rasheera Dopson watched each fluorescent light as it came and went from her line of sight. The medical team was wheeling Rasheera into the operating room for yet another surgery—number 102 in only twenty-six years of life.

Rasheera was feeling the effects of the calming medication, and the world around her started to shift out of focus. She was still coherent, though; she knew the arduous task that would begin once she reached the operating room. All too soon the metal sides of the gurney were lowered and Rasheera's body was lifted and transferred onto the operating table. She continued her silent prayers for strength and protection.

A month prior, Rasheera had been in the same spot waiting for the same surgery, but when the anesthesiologist tried to intubate her, first through her mouth and then her nose, Rasheera's throat closed up and she stopped breathing. The doctors immediately aborted the surgery. Rasheera remained unresponsive for quite some time, and when she finally awakened, she coughed up massive amounts of blood. Her face throbbed; her chest and throat felt as though they were on fire. Worst of all, Rasheera realized she still suffered from the very pain in her jaw that had led her to the surgery in the first place. She almost lost her life on the operating table, and the surgery was abandoned before anyone could alleviate the excruciating pain that had tormented Rasheera for months. To eliminate the discomfort, she would need to attempt the surgery again.

Now, Rasheera was about to face the same threat of death, but this time she was acutely aware of the risks. In most surgeries, patients are intubated after they fall asleep, but for this attempt, the anesthesiologist opted to keep Rasheera awake. This allowed him to monitor Rasheera's breathing and ensure that she breathed on her own as the tube was inserted. Rasheera's throat and nose had been numbed to ease the discomfort, but nothing could completely eliminate the feeling of a foreign object snaking its way down her trachea. The doctors first attempted to intubate Rasheera through her mouth, but after thirty minutes without success, they switched to her nose.

Rasheera continued to stare up at the bright overhead light as the doctors worked to insert the tube. She focused on the Christian music playing in the background and on the nurse who held her hand for comfort. Rasheera continued to pray for protection as the tube slowly found its way down her narrow trachea. She swallowed to aid in the tube's movement, and it finally fell into in place. As another tube was inserted, she choked and gasped; her ability to breathe had been blocked, but by what she did not know. In that moment, she froze. But as quickly as her breathing was impaired, it came back. Only then did Rasheera drift off into the deepest sleep anesthesia could provide.

Rasheera remembers, "It had been eight years since my last surgery. I had forgotten all the nervousness that goes into going under the knife. It was in that moment that I realized how vulnerable having an operation could be. When I was younger, I feared that vulnerability; as I got older, I realized that very vulnerability could be my greatest strength."

* * *

One hundred two: That is the number of surgeries Rasheera has had during her short lifetime. She grew up more comfortable in a hospital room than in a classroom. The hospital almost felt like a second home to her, a place where she was looked after and cared for.

Rasheera was born prematurely on June 5, 1991, and weighed only fifteen ounces. Her body was extremely underdeveloped as a result of being born at only thirty-one weeks. Her organs did not have time to fully form in the womb, which created concern about their functionality. Her kidneys were a major worry, because newborns cannot survive with missing or nonfunctioning kidneys. Rasheera was attached to life support and everyone waited to see how she would handle her first forty-eight hours, the most crucial for newborns under duress. No one knew if she would live through her first night.

Sometime after midnight, a nurse came running into Rasheera's mother's hospital room screaming, "She peed!

She peed! She's going to live!" It was the critical sign the medical staff had been waiting for, proof that Rasheera not only had kidneys, but also that they were working. Still, Rasheera faced a difficult road, which began with spending the first few months of her life in a hospital until she was strong enough to be discharged.

While hospitalized after her birth, Rasheera was diagnosed with VATER syndrome, a condition consisting of five abnormalities that typically occur in conjunction with one another. VATER is an acronym for the vertebrae, anus, trachea, esophagus, and renal system (kidneys), all of which are affected by birth defects. In 1991, Rasheera became only the seventh person in the United States to be diagnosed with VATER syndrome, though today it affects roughly one in 40,000 people.

Not every person diagnosed with VATER syndrome exhibits birth defects in all five areas, but in order to be diagnosed, a child must have birth defects in at least three. Rasheera was not born with problematic kidneys, but she did have complications pertaining to the other four components of the syndrome. She had fused vertebrae in her spine that limited the mobility of her back and neck. She was born without anal and vaginal openings. The only reason her doctor knew she was a female was because she had ovaries. Rasheera used a colostomy bag for years, until doctors could construct an anal orifice for bowel movements. The last two parts of the syndrome that afflicted Rasheera were the T and E, which were related. She suffered from tracheoesophageal fistula, a condition that connected the trachea (windpipe) and the esophagus (the tube that carries food to the stomach). Normally, the trachea and esophagus remain separate; when they join, as in Rasheera's case, food can divert into the lungs rather than traveling to the stomach.

Rasheera's mother would soon find that VATER syndrome was not the only condition affecting the development of her daughter's body. Rasheera also was diagnosed with Goldenhar syndrome and Hemifacial Microsomia, two related craniofacial conditions. While VATER affected Rasheera's internal organs, Goldenhar and Hemifacial Microsomia had more visible traits. Characteristics of Goldenhar syndrome typically included missing or malformed ears, underdeveloped facial features affecting only one side of the face, heart defects, growths on the eye, and spinal deformities. Consistent with those syndromes, the right side of Rasheera's face appeared crooked, as if it never fully formed in the womb. Her bone structure on that side, including the jaw, was underdeveloped, and she was missing her right ear. This facial asymmetry correlated to Hemifacial Microsomia, which was one of the indications of Goldenhar syndrome. (By definition, a syndrome is a group of symptoms that always appear together.) Rasheera's heart condition and fused vertebrae were two other symptoms of Goldenhar that also were associated with VATER. Rasheera ultimately would be diagnosed with multiple rare conditions, all of which were intertwined.

When people look at Rasheera now as an adult, they usually notice her facial differences and presume that is the extent of her medical issues. In reality, however, her craniofacial condition affected her life far less than her VATER syndrome. Her internal anomalies proved much more problematic, because they directly affected her ability to live. Rasheera could not perform basic daily functions such as eating or defecating without the help of medical equipment. Her growth and survival depended on invasive reconstructive operations, the first of which occurred when she was only eighteen hours old. That surgery allowed doctors to explore her organs and repair some of the issues with her heart, lungs, and bowels. This was also when doctors confirmed that Rasheera's kidneys were indeed intact and fully functioning.

By the time she was six years old, Rasheera had undergone sixty-nine surgeries, fifty-two of which had been to her digestive system, which her doctors had to rebuild because she was born with only half a stomach. There was a period in her life when Rasheera had an operation every six to eight weeks. Other surgeries included open-heart surgery to close the hole in her heart, surgeries to create openings for her anus and vagina, jaw reconstruction, and ear reconstruction. The surgeons concentrated first on the reconstruction of her internal systems. Each surgery was painful but necessary.

Rasheera's childhood was full of doctor visits, hospital stays, and unanswered questions. Because she was born very prematurely, Rasheera had a weak immune system, which left her chronically ill. There always seemed to be a new mystery to solve with her health. Most of the time, doctors could identify her symptoms but couldn't offer a complete diagnosis. She had so many issues with her body that it was impossible to draw definite medical conclusions. Even when doctors could officially diagnose Rasheera with an illness, they did not always know how, or if, she could be healed.

Reflecting on her youth, Rasheera says, "My childhood was great, although complicated. My early years were consumed by my sickness. While I was too young to remember every single operation, I felt the weight of my illness. My family never really dealt with the psychological effects of what I was enduring; we just pressed through it. My mom had been the person standing by my side through all the operations, and I rarely saw her cry. Years later I learned that when a doctor casually mentioned to her how all I ever knew was pain from the moment I was born, she broke down in tears in his office. She felt sorry for me because she didn't want to think her baby could be suffering. But I'm here. I'm alive. My family was my rock through everything."

When she was five years old, Rasheera experienced a prolonged bout of nausea and vomiting and was diagnosed with another rare condition known as Cyclic Vomiting syndrome (CVS). This syndrome affects young children more than adults and is difficult to diagnose, because so many different factors can cause vomiting. Rasheera would feel nauseated and vomit repeatedly for weeks at a time with no sense of relief. Often, the vomiting would become so intense she would need to be hospitalized two or three times a month. She would violently vomit up blood and bile. She would lie in her hospital bed, weak from dehydration, while nurses tried desperately to find a vein to pump fluids into her body. When Rasheera would run a dangerously high fever, her mother would either lay cool towels all over her body or place her in a bathtub full of cold water in hopes the fever would break quickly. If it didn't, Rasheera faced the possibility of seizures. It seemed that whenever Rasheera wasn't undergoing an operation for her VATER or Goldenhar syndromes, she was hospitalized because of her CVS.

Many of Rasheera's most complex surgeries occurred when she was too young to remember, which has been for the best. She accumulated enough negative memories over the years and didn't need to add to her list of horrors. She lived with the possibility of being transported back to the hospital at the drop of a hat. If she closed her eyes, her senses would immediately be flooded with reminders of her surgeries, sometimes triggered by sights, smells, and sounds. She could visualize the buckets of vomit next to her bedside. She could feel the nurses pricking her skin over and over, searching for a vein to draw blood or insert an IV catheter. She could smell the distinctive odor of the anesthesia being forced into her lungs.

The vivid memory of the mask being placed on her face haunted her the most. She never knew what condition she would be in when she woke up after her operations, and that frightened her. During her ninety-ninth surgery, doctors intubated her improperly. Rasheera went into respiratory failure during the surgery and almost died. She awoke in the recovery room gasping for air. She struggled to breathe on her own. Nurses covered her nose and mouth with a mask and forced oxygen into her lungs until she was finally stabilized.

Rasheera doesn't mind having zero recollection of the worst surgeries she's faced because she has enough emotional baggage from the operations she *does* remember.

"I imagine that how I feel about my surgeries now, especially after the one hundred second surgery, is almost like PTSD," she says. "I've obviously had more operations than I can recall, but certain aspects are haunting. The memories aren't something that will fade with time; they'll always be there. However, I'm more affected by those memories as an adult because I have the maturity level to really understand the weight of everything I experienced."

For Rasheera, one of the hardest parts of being chronically ill was the impact it had on her ability to succeed in school. It seemed that when she wasn't undergoing or recovering from a surgery, she was being hospitalized for her Cyclic Vomiting. Because she spent more time in the hospital or at home in recovery than she did in a classroom, Rasheera fell behind in her studies. By the time she reached middle school and realized just how advanced her classmates were, it was too late. Her teachers had let her coast through elementary school without considering the future ramifications of her not comprehending basic math and grammar concepts.

Even as Rasheera's surgeries grew less frequent and she was able to spend more time in school, the education system did not have a plan to help students like her, those who missed too much schooling due to illness but did not have any kind of cognitive impairment. Rasheera was smart; she just needed help catching up to the rest of her classmates because she had missed so much school in the early years. Before she started eleventh grade, Rasheera and her family moved to a new town. On her first day of school, she saw she had a class called "Study Skills" but did not think much of it. She found her classroom and chose a seat. Something seemed different about this class, but she couldn't quite place it. When the class began, her teacher passed out the day's assignment. As Rasheera looked down at the math problem on the page, she was livid. The class was learning simple addition: 2+2=4. Rasheera had been placed into a special-education class.

Rasheera was accustomed to having an Individualized Education Program (IEP), which set specific goals for her based on her individual needs. She understood that she had some academic delays due to missing so much school, but the IEP was supposed to help Rasheera fill in some of the gaps in her education. Somehow when the advisor at her new school saw Rasheera's medical history and need for an IEP, she assumed Rasheera was developmentally delayed. As soon as the bell rang, Rasheera stormed out of the classroom and explained her situation to her advisor.

Even after being placed in regular classes, though, the stigma of being intellectually inferior followed Rasheera. Her teachers constantly reminded her that she wasn't as smart as her peers. She was told she was too far behind and would never catch up. One teacher was so bold as to tell her that colleges would never accept her. Teachers did not express any confidence that Rasheera could succeed in life, and their comments filled her with self-doubt.

"I felt defeated all of the time," Rasheera recalls. "It was a very frustrating time. It's like my education was some sort of physical barrier and I didn't know how to navigate it. I couldn't simply 'jump over' this barrier because I had a disability, and my educators really couldn't understand that. Deep down, I knew I had the power to be somebody, but I didn't have the self-confidence to obtain it at the time."

Rasheera did not need her teachers to place any more doubt into her head. She had plenty of self-esteem issues as a side effect of dealing with physical differences. In third grade, Rasheera had begun to feel more self-conscious about her crooked face and missing ear. Her classmates pointed and stared at her abnormalities and began to tease her. It did not help that her family moved frequently, and her arrival at each new school amplified her insecurities. In addition to the physical complications of her syndromes, Rasheera was having to deal with the emotional side effects, as well. That meant facing a newly acquired fear: rejection.

Rasheera's sense of rejection deepened as she grew older. Once her surgeries began to dwindle when she was around the age of nine or ten, Rasheera found herself facing new territory. Though the hospital carried many of her most traumatic memories, it was also a source of familiarity. Rasheera found that her identity relied heavily on her medical history. Her church community regarded her as the "miracle child" because of everything she'd endured. To her classmates, she was the girl who fluttered in and out of school, though they never really grasped why. Rasheera didn't know how to be anything else.

She spent so much time alone in the hospital that her social skills had not developed. She didn't know how to fit in, so she isolated herself. She longed to have friends, but at the same time, she shut herself off from her peers. Rasheera intentionally created barriers and avoided social interactions. She did not know how to talk to her peers about her medical conditions, so she never let anyone get close enough to want to know more about her. Even if they did want to know more, she feared they would not stick around after she had her next operation. She'd experienced that kind of rejection in the past and was certain she would be left alone once again.

Rasheera explains: "My isolation was self-inflicted and I let it torture me. I used to love pep rallies at school. The vibe was so incredible; all of my peers gathered together in celebration created such an electric energy. But as much as I loved the intensity of those events, I stopped going. I would imagine walking into the auditorium alone without having anyone to sit and talk to. I didn't want anyone to point out that I didn't have any friends. Instead of risking embarrassment, I skipped out on one of my favorite activities."

As an adult, Rasheera held on to the insecurities she developed in her youth. She guarded her heart, still unsure how to be anything other than a chronically ill child. Her circumstances seemed to define her. She constantly wondered if people looking at her judged her by her appearance and if anyone would ask what had happened to her face. She thought back to the times when her family would run into people they hadn't seen in a while. Those people would fawn over Rasheera's sister, commenting, "Oh, you're such a pretty young lady!" Then they would turn to Rasheera and sigh, saying, "And you're so strong." Rasheera considered her strength a necessity in overcoming her medical obstacles; she did not have any other choice but to be strong if she wanted to survive. Deep inside, however, she wished that just once someone would tell her she was pretty, too.

Rasheera knew she looked different. She saw it every time she glanced in the mirror. She purposely wore her hair down to cover the unevenness of her face and the scarring from her reconstructive surgeries. She wanted to be more than what she saw in the mirror. She wanted someone to tell her she was pretty—not strong, not courageous, not even pretty special, just pretty.

"I've found that there is a standard of beauty for females in this world. We're expected to have perfect features, perfect hair, perfect teeth, and even have a keen sense of fashion. I was the complete opposite of that standard," Rasheera says. "Yes, sometimes I thought I was cute, but it was never the same; *pretty* wasn't a word that people often used to compliment me. I wanted to hear someone say that, despite my imperfections, I was beautiful."

These insecurities toyed with Rasheera's emotions even after the bulk of her operations were in the past. She was used to being a medical marvel and never quite understood who she was without that label. She did not know how to separate herself from the syndromes that controlled her life.

In 2016, Rasheera attended a women's group meeting at her church, and the topic of their discussion was confidence. Rasheera asked her pastor, "What if you have low self-esteem and insecurities? How can you move past them?" Her pastor looked at her and told her to find out what caused her insecurities and then find a way to use them to her advantage.

Rasheera put herself on a mission to gain the sense of confidence that had always eluded her. She determined that her insecurities stemmed from her not comprehending her surgeries and how they affected her life. Because she was so young when most of her surgeries occurred, she never fully grasped what her syndromes meant and what they'd caused her to endure. She never knew how to answer people when they asked her questions about her condition. Worse, she couldn't answer those same questions for herself. Rasheera knew that if she wanted to begin healing, she needed to fully understand her medical history.

Until that point, she hadn't been open to discussing her past. But her syndrome had defined who she was, and she had to get to the root of what was holding her back. Rasheera decided to call the Oakland (California) Children's Hospital and request her medical records. When she received the records in the mail, Rasheera was flabbergasted to see such a large stack of papers. She sat down on the floor ready to confront her insecurities. When she read the record that said she'd had sixty-nine surgeries by the time she was six years old, her body crumbled in disbelief. At that time, she was a substitute teacher for second-graders and could not imagine seeing a child that small endure as much as she had. That realization sent Rasheera on a two-day crying fit. She realized she had suppressed the memories from when she was very young and had compartmentalized the emotions that went along with those memories. Reading her medical records left her feeling overwhelmed but also set her on the path of healing.

As Rasheera read through her medical history, she realized she had no reason to be ashamed of anything in her past. The knowledge she gained during that process not only helped her understand the complexity of her life but also granted her a newfound freedom to be herself. Now, she lives her life entirely confident. She owns her uniqueness and her entire medical experience. When she catches someone staring, she embraces the gaze. She is confident in herself and in the person she has become.

"Getting my medical records was sobering in many ways. Over the years, so many people have indirectly discounted my surgeries. You'd be surprised," Rasheera says. "Most people think it's unbelievable when they hear the number of surgeries I've had; they look at me and don't understand the reason why I've had so many. Some people think my operations were for purely cosmetic reasons, but that wasn't the case at all. Out of my one hundred two surgeries, I only had about twenty related to my face. Most of my surgeries were 100 percent necessary for me to be able to live a typical life. I've heard people judge my mom for allowing doctors to put me through so much. But my condition was beyond my mom's control; it was out of anyone's control. Even though I knew this, I began taking to heart the doubts that so many people had. I began to question my surgeries. However, when I saw the medical records for myself and read all of the doctors' comments, it silenced every negative voice in my head. Seeing my records helped me to embrace my truth, and once I did that, I began to see my life differently. Rather than being ashamed or uncertain of my past, I now know it's a powerful story that I have the privilege of telling."

Rasheera understands that her life will always be filled with complications, and she will always be cognizant of the ways in which she is different from everyone else. If a problem arises, her solution might be far more difficult than it would be for the vast majority of people. For example, her last surgery, number 102, would not have been necessary for anyone else. Rasheera had been experiencing excruciating pain in her teeth and visited her dentist to find answers. The dentist examined her teeth and found that Rasheera had one cracked tooth and five others that were severely infected. For a typical patient, this would have resulted in either a root canal or tooth extraction done under local anesthesia. It is a relatively simple process for someone who does not have brittle bone structure.

But Rasheera's dentist was unfamiliar with Goldenhar syndrome and referred Rasheera to an oral surgeon who she thought would be better equipped to handle Rasheera's unique jaw structure. But even the oral surgeon feared he would cause harm to Rasheera's delicate jawbone. Rasheera was then sent on a hunt to find a plastic surgeon who could handle the removal of her infected teeth. Once she did, she was told she would be placed under general anesthesia as a precaution because of fears that her jawbone might break during surgery. A situation that would have had a simple solution for anyone without a craniofacial condition turned out to almost cost Rasheera her life.

Having always turned to writing as a form of therapy, Rasheera wrote a memoir about her life's experiences titled *Dying 101 Times: A Journey of Hope, Healing and Restoration*. She realized the only way for people to learn about her conditions was if she shared the unfiltered truth about her life.

Not only does she want to inspire people through her writing, she aims to become a motivational speaker and host conferences for young women with a focus on confidence and self-esteem. Rasheera also created an online community known as Beauties with a Twist. The message of the community is that no matter your circumstances, you can overcome the odds. Often, people who are different have a mind-set that they are broken. Rasheera aims to change that by creating a community in which people can be exactly who they are and learn to see themselves in a healthy light.

If you met Rasheera today, you would think she had always been a confident and self-assured young lady. But she used to suffer from depression and feel isolated. She acknowledges that she needed to shift her mind-set in order to blossom into her confidence, and that this mind-set is a lifelong focus for her. As she grows stronger, her story changes. She encourages everyone she meets to embrace their stories, to love their flaws, and to be different. And she reminds everyone that just because others might place limitations on you, you do not have to place those same limitations on yourself. Rasheera, after being told she wasn't smart enough to go to college, graduated with a bachelor's degree in English. She is currently pursuing her master's degree in communications with a specialization in journalism.

"When I look back over my life, I am amazed," she says. "I'm totally in awe seeing how far I've come and knowing how far I will go. I think my story is important to tell because it gives hope. I feel like that is the theme of my life, really. There were moments where my condition offered no signs of hope, but somehow, I surpassed them. I don't take that for granted. I used to see myself as a little black girl who was a nobody; now through confidence and empowerment, I can see that I am somebody and my story is worth sharing with the world."

Rasheera continually reminds us never to accept the labels that others force upon us. In a time when strong voices need to be heard, Rasheera Dopson is the perfect advocate for embracing one's differences and finding confidence. She won't let anything or anyone stop her from breaking down barriers.

If you'd like to support an organization close to Rasheera's heart, please visit the Children's Craniofacial Association at ccakids.org.

Jaime

On paper, small towns in central Illinois seem to be the ideal places to raise a family, but for Jaime Smith, suburban living almost cost her her life. She was, as she puts it, the girl who had it all. She was a thirty-six-year-old married mom with four kids aged eight to eighteen, and ten years prior she had snagged her dream job as a high-powered marketing manager. On the surface, Jaime's life seemed nothing but enviable. But behind the scenes, her life was anything but a perfect snapshot.

In 2013, Jaime and her new husband, Chuck, purchased a home together in a small, upscale town where neither of them had lived before. Both had children from previous relationships, and this new town was in a great school district. The blended family was creating a promising new life together.

But the new beginnings came to a crashing halt one September day when Jaime's family suffered a tragic loss: her stepson's mother and Chuck's ex-wife, Jen, passed away from metastatic breast cancer. Though it was not an unexpected passing, it was heartbreaking for the family.

Leading up to her death, Jen had been very vocal about her battle with stage four cancer. She wrote two books, appeared on *The Ellen DeGeneres Show*, and was featured in numerous articles about living with cancer. She made it a point to put her story in the media on a regular basis to show women they could continue to live positively even after a cancer diagnosis. Being the new wife to Jen's ex-husband, Jaime found herself exposed to the public's scrutiny. It came with the territory since Jen repeatedly mentioned the "bad marriage" she'd exited after being diagnosed with cancer.

The local news stations and papers covered Jen's passing in 2013. The media also focused on how Jen's son, who lived with Jaime and Chuck, was coping. Because of the attention her family received, Jaime felt as if she were being judged for how she reacted to Jen's passing. If she was caught crying about her own problems, people thought she was being selfish. If she wasn't crying, people thought she was cold and uncaring. It didn't matter whether Jaime controlled her emotions or let them run rampant. She didn't know to react, but she knew she had to remain resilient for the four children she had at home, one whose mother had just passed away.

Everywhere Jaime went, people would come up to talk to her about her personal situation, which also included an already rocky marriage. Though Jaime and Chuck had dated for several years, they'd rushed to the altar to reassure Jen her son would be well cared for after her passing. The couple fulfilled Jen's dying wish, but the sudden nuptials strained Jaime and Chuck's relationship. And Jaime's oldest son was falling in with the wrong crowd at his new school, which became a topic of gossip as well. Jaime felt worthless, as though she were failing as a wife and mother. It seemed as if nothing she did was good enough.

"People don't realize how bad gossip, finger-pointing, and whispering hurt people. I wish people could have compassion and simply not be mean to others," Jaime says.

The pressure of having every detail of her life unfold before the public became too much for Jaime to bear.

Depression and anxiety controlled her life. After consulting with some friends who were on antidepressants and anti-anxiety medication, Jaime thought the symptoms she displayed mirrored those of her friends. Once Jaime realized she could no longer function in an agitated, apprehensive state, she visited her doctor, who prescribed Xanax and Zoloft.

Prior to Jen's death, Jaime had befriended some of the other mothers with whom her kids went to school and played sports. These women had heard about what was happening to Jaime's family and took notice of how her demeanor changed. Jaime seemed to be constantly on edge. When the women mentioned to Jaime that they noticed the changes in her personality, she admitted she was on medication to ease her anxiety but still found herself suffering from insomnia. These women had a solution for Jaime: They introduced her to hydrocodone and assured her it would help her sleep better. Jaime had taken hydrocodone in the past after surgeries, and indeed it had helped her sleep through the night. So, when the other mothers offered her the pills, she didn't think it was a big deal. After all, the prescription had been written by someone's doctor, and Jaime had used the drugs before without any issues. Jaime quickly came to learn that these soccer moms stockpiled various prescription medications. Hydrocodone, an opioid with mood-affecting tendencies, was just one of many.

Within a month of adding hydrocodone to her daily routine of pills, Jaime was addicted. She had found a medication that allowed her to rest, and she feared stopping it would cause her to revert to being agitated and sleep-deprived. She also felt she could function better while taking the pills because she focused more on the needs of her children instead of her own stressors. From that point on, she joined what she calls "a pill gang of suburban housewives." This "gang" would doctor-shop together in the neighboring towns and cities. They each visited separate doctors complaining of different symptoms to acquire whatever pills they could get their hands on, such as Percocet, Xanax, OxyContin, and methadone. Jaime had hoped to find a way to escape her personal tragedies, but her means of escape quickly became a dangerous addiction.

By 2015, Jaime still found herself to be the center of unwanted attention from the people in her town. Her family life had not improved, and neighbors gossiped about how they thought Jaime's marriage would fail and how she had trouble controlling her children. (Her oldest son was still socializing with a bad crowd.) Jaime felt that everywhere she went in her town, people were judging what seemed to be her failures. To make matters worse, Jaime's beloved grandfather passed away during this time. He had always been her biggest supporter, and the loss was more than Jaime could bear. There did not appear to be an end in sight for the heartache that kept Jaime trapped. All she wanted was her life back, but all she continued to find were bottles of medication.

Nearly two years after her first dose of prescription relief, Jaime depended on the pills to function. Opioids like hydrocodone alter the chemicals in the brain, and after constant use, the body comes to rely on the drugs to feel even remotely normal.

Jaime continued to hide her addiction from her family. Her husband had not noticed any excessive or unexplainable purchases because Jaime had her own bank account and made a great salary. If Chuck or one of the children saw Jaime taking a pill and asked what it was, she would nonchalantly tell them it was just a Tylenol. Her family believed her, and why wouldn't they? They had no reason to suspect she was on drugs. They hadn't noticed any changes in her daily demeanor to suggest otherwise.

One day, tired of the constant pressure she received from every angle of her life, Jaime quit her job. Her company had just undergone a reorganization, and Jaime's new position demanded more travel than ever before. Jaime could no longer tolerate the schedule and deadlines her job required. Without considering the ramifications of leaving a job before securing a new one, she put in her two-week notice. Jaime finally had reached a point where her prescription drug use had started to affect her life. Looking back on it, Jaime says she realizes that had she not been under the influence at the time, she would not have quit her job without truly thinking it through.

Jaime's family was still oblivious to her drug use and attributed this spontaneous decision to a midlife crisis. The family had plenty of money in savings, and Jaime leaving her job did not put a dent in their lifestyle.

Of course, the other mothers in the pill gang knew the truth about Jaime. They noticed her addiction growing out of control. Jaime wrecked her car in an accident, began to arrive chronically late to places, and was hiding her pill stash from the other mothers. Jaime was no longer a functioning addict, someone who discreetly abused drugs without disrupting her normal life. Once Jaime quit her job, her façade of normality began to deteriorate.

Fearing her changing behavior would eventually expose their own drug use, the other mothers kicked Jaime out of their gang. Having lost her connection to a wide range of prescription drugs, Jaime turned to a cheaper, more easily accessible drug to prevent her from going through withdrawal: heroin.

Jaime was first introduced to harder, illegal drugs like heroin and cocaine by the other mothers in her pill gang shortly before she was kicked out. They slowly began incorporating these harder drugs into their daily fixes for various reasons: the high lasted longer, the cost was significantly lower than prescription pills, and the access to these drugs was much easier since they found out some of the local high school students were dealers. Once Jaime found a dealer, a package of heroin would show up on her doorstep while the rest of the family was out of the house. It seemed to be an effortless process compared to that of doctor-shopping for prescription pills.

Like many users, Jaime first snorted heroin, which yielded a high within ten to fifteen minutes. How quickly the effects of the drug can be felt depends on the method of delivery. For a quicker high, users graduate to intramuscular injection, which takes five to eight minutes to generate effects, and intravenous injection, which takes a mere seven to eight seconds. Within three weeks, Jaime was a full-blown IV heroin user. She also began shooting cocaine to counterbalance the noticeable effects of the heroin while remaining in the euphoric state of a high. Heroin is a depressant and lulls the user into a sedated state by slowing respiration; cocaine, on the other hand, is a stimulant and elicits feelings of increased energy and elevated mood. Even though Jaime had shifted to harder drugs, the pairing of a depressant and a stimulant allowed her to function normally and helped keep her addiction hidden from her family. In fact, the drug use helped her hide an entire secret life.

After quitting her job, Jaime began doing contract work that required her to travel to Chicago frequently. In September 2015, during one of these work trips to the city, Jaime met a man who loved drugs as much as she did and who fed her addiction. She would stay with this man whenever she was in Chicago, even lying to Chuck by telling him she had meetings in the city when she didn't. Five months into the relationship, Jaime's boyfriend beat her severely; only then did Chuck find out about the affair.

Chuck had begun to suspect something was wrong with his wife when her trips to Chicago turned more frequent, but he never suspected drugs. After Chuck learned about the affair, Jaime confided in him about her pill addiction—but she did not mention her dependence on heroin or cocaine.

"I remember looking in the mirror and no longer recognizing the girl staring back at me," Jaime says. "I dropped thirty pounds and was skin and bones, with no light in my eyes. I would stare at my reflection asking myself what had happened to me."

Yet nothing shook Jaime from her drug-induced stupor. She left Chuck and their four children at the end of February 2016—after about a year of using heroin—and moved to Chicago to live with her drug-dealing boyfriend. Despite her boyfriend's abusive tendencies, Jaime felt like he understood her and her reliance on drugs.

Even in the wake of Jaime's cheating and deceit, Chuck did not give up on their relationship. In March, he called Jaime and begged her to drive home from Chicago so they could talk. Jaime was ashamed of the person she had become over the last three years. She already had lost herself and was afraid of losing her husband and children as well. She agreed and returned home to her family. Deep down, Jaime knew she needed help, but at the same time, she couldn't part with the drugs that were ruining her life. On the drive home to her family, she wondered how soon she would be able to get her next fix.

As soon as she arrived at home, Jaime exposed the full extent of her drug addiction to Chuck. She had been afraid to open up to him about the details, but his unflinching reaction suggested he had put the pieces together after learning about her addiction to pills.

Chuck was intent on finding help for his wife and began researching various treatment centers. Two days later, he had a sizable list and feverishly called each one to see if there was a place for Jaime. As her husband made the phone calls, Jaime stared at her reflection in the bathroom mirror and thought, *What are people going to say about me if I admit I have a problem and ask for help? Who is going to hire me for another job? What are people going to say to my children? What are they going to say to my husband?*

With those thoughts swarming in her brain, Jaime decided to take her own life by overdosing.

But, found unconscious on the bathroom floor by a family member after only five minutes, Jaime was rushed to a hospital, given Narcan, and revived. Chuck urged her to seek help and she relented. Jaime finally had realized she could not continue to live this double life. It would kill her; it might even destroy her entire family as the truth unfolded.

In April 2016, two days after her hospital stint, Jaime checked in to an inpatient treatment facility where she remained for thirty days. She underwent seven days of intense detox when it felt like she had the stomach flu, but ten times worse. Jaime had become chemically dependent on drugs, and weaning her off that dependency was torture. Because she had been consistently using various drugs for almost three years, she had developed a high tolerance for those substances, which made her detoxification process especially intense. As the substances exited her body and she entered into withdrawal, Jaime suffered from body aches, chills, muscle spasms, and vomiting. "It was hell," Jaime recalls. "The pain was worse than childbirth."

The process of withdrawal also affected her emotionally, a common response for people battling substance abuse. Jaime was terrified of detoxing. She became belligerent; she yelled at everyone who was trying to help her and even started physical fights. Jaime's conscience told her to get clean, but her mind and body craved the drugs. Once the last of the drugs left Jaime's system, her withdrawal symptoms stabilized. The process drained her, but Jaime was one step closer to living a clean life.

When she completed the seven-day detox, Jaime began the rehabilitation portion of her stay at the center and began a series of group and one-on-one counseling sessions. At first, she resisted the help. She wished she could be getting high instead of sitting in a room with people who wanted to help her reclaim sobriety. She didn't want to be there, didn't want to participate. Eventually, though, Jaime's mindset shifted after she met a counselor who expressed faith in her recovery. The counselor actively listened to Jaime and helped her come to terms with the mistakes she had made. Once she accepted the program and understood its teachings, Jaime surrendered to treatment and benefited from being there. She learned coping skills for her anxiety and depression, and even more importantly, she learned how to forgive herself, something she needed to do in order to heal. Jaime stayed in the inpatient center for thirty days and then completed a ninety-day outpatient program.

Jaime now has been clean for more than two years. She admits that her addiction and recovery have been very hard on her entire family. On drugs, she acted in ways that were uncharacteristic for her; she never would have cheated on her husband or left her family had she not been under the influence. Jaime feels she poisoned her family and they've had to get healthy together little by little. Jaime's children found out about her addiction when they visited her in treatment, and they were devastated by the news. Even though Jaime was the person hooked on drugs, her entire family is in recovery. Their relationships were tested and broken by Jaime's actions while under the influence; now, the family is working together to salvage the wreckage and rebuild their trust in one another.

Jaime realizes that recovery is forever. Her rehabilitation did not end after her three months of outpatient care concluded. Even now, she visits a therapist once a week and attends a weekly group recovery program. This continued process has taught Jaime to trust her inner strength. Recovery is a daily undertaking, but Jaime has come to realize the key to success is to focus on the present. On those not-so-great days or when Jaime hears people gossiping about her, the voice in her mind tells her, "Numb it. Jaime, just numb it. Take a pill and numb it." But she knows she can't do that. Treatment gave her the tools and resources to live in recovery. Treatment did not cure Jaime's addiction; it educated her about her addiction.

Jaime and her family still live in the same community that aided in her fall from grace. Jaime refuses to run away. By staying, she hopes to teach her children that when people make mistakes, they must own up to their wrongdoings, stand tall, and make their lives right again. Of course, remaining in her small community means Jaime still finds herself confronted by her pill-popping past. She sees the other mothers from her pill gang around town, though they mostly avoid her. While Jaime is in recovery, the others still battle with their secret addictions. One day at her daughter's volleyball game, Jaime walked in on one of the mothers snorting a line of cocaine in the bathroom. The woman offered her some, but Jaime ran from the bathroom to put distance between herself and the old habits that almost killed her.

Looking back, Jaime wishes her local doctor had referred her to a psychologist instead of pushing medication on her right from the start. She openly shares her story now because she realizes many people do not understand that drugs do not discriminate.

"I chose to speak out for several reasons," Jaime says. "The first was to own my mistakes. My life was put in the public eye, and everywhere I went, people were talking about me, so I decided to own my story and tell it from my own mouth. This was my opportunity to stand up, own my mistakes, tell my story, and slowly rebuild my life. I also speak out because addiction is happening everywhere. These days, everyone knows someone who might have a problem with drugs or alcohol. I want to show people that addiction does not discriminate and that it can happen to anyone at any time. I also wanted to show those struggling that there is a way out and that they can get better."

Before becoming involved with drugs herself, Jaime never would have imagined a small suburban town could be the gateway to addiction. She's not alone. Most people would have a hard time believing that soccer moms pop and swap pills to get high. But the truth is addiction happens everywhere, not just in cities or back alleys.

A study published in *JAMA Psychiatry* in May 2014 found that the demographic for heroin users has shifted since the 1960s. The study found that a staggering 75 percent of heroin users lived outside the urban setting, destroying the perception that drug use exists only in the inner cities. Fifty years ago, heroin use was found to be equally prevalent across people of various races. Today, 90 percent of users are Caucasian, most of whom first began taking prescription opioid pills to relieve stress or pain symptoms; they then graduated to heroin because opioid pills became heavily monitored. Heroin became easier to find, cost less, and provided an even better high than the pills. According to the research, roughly 52 percent of heroin addicts are women; much like Jaime, many are mothers trying to manage the pressures of their lives, and drugs fill voids they didn't know existed.

Jaime's biggest piece of advice for someone struggling with life the way she did is to first visit a psychologist before trying prescription pills for anxiety or depression. Prior to her addiction, Jaime watched television shows like *Intervention* and wondered why addicts couldn't simply stop taking the pills they were hooked on. But, as she found out, opioids not only take away physical pain, they also numb mental pain. They create artificial endorphins in the brain, leaving the user with an elevated mood. Of course, the body develops a tolerance for the drugs over time, and to counteract that, the user is forced to increase the doses. Thus, an addiction is born. When you're going through an emotional trauma, it becomes very easy to crave the elimination of pain. You quickly become dependent on that release to survive.

"Once the high wears off, you're going to deal with your reality again," Jaime explains.

Jaime wants anyone struggling with addiction to know this: "If I can get better, anybody can. There is life after addiction. You can get your life back. It's not easy, but you can do it."

Jaime has turned her experiences with addiction into a positive. She hopes to shed light on the growing opioid epidemic and let others who might be struggling know they are not alone.

"My strength comes from my husband, family, and friends who have been by my side before, during, and after addiction," Jaime says, "the people who never gave up on me and who refused to walk away and who remain by my side still today."

Jaime now advocates for addiction awareness. She has told her story to local news outlets and online publications in hopes of shattering the stigma that substance addiction happens only to a certain group of people. With no genetic predisposition to substance abuse and having used opioids after surgeries in the past without issue, Jaime warns that these addictions can happen to anyone; she is proof of that. Jaime also meets with politicians to discuss the opioid epidemic, mentors addicts wanting to change their lives, and speaks at schools about the dangers of drug use. Jaime knows firsthand how high school students are at the forefront of the drug epidemic. Some of her own town's teenagers used to supply Jaime and her pill gang with hydrocodone and heroin.

Jaime hopes to educate the public about this epidemic before it's too late. According to the Centers for Disease Control and Prevention, ninety-one people lose their lives to opioid addiction each day. Jaime feels fortunate not to have fallen into that statistic.

Jaime has found her voice by candidly sharing her story. By mustering the courage to speak about her opioid addiction, she understands her life has come full circle and that recovery is one of her greatest achievements. Another of Jaime's achievements was being listed as a success story on the website of her treatment center.

"I have had many accomplishments in my life, but this is by far the most rewarding because I was convinced that my addiction would take my life," Jaime says. "People don't realize how hard recovery really is, and to be publicly acknowledged for it on the Prairie Center website means the world to me. It allows me to show others that addiction doesn't have to define you and that you can get your life back."

Jaime's story is a reminder that adversity does not have to define who we are. Through determination and with the help of others, we can reclaim our lives after our darkest hours and inspire others who feel alone in their struggles. By doing that, Jaime Smith has admirably found her way from heroin to heroine.

....

If you'd like to support an organization close to Jaime's heart, please visit the Prairie Center, now called Rosecrance, at rosecrance.org.

Camille

Many people cannot fathom caring for even one child who requires special attention. In fact, before the birth of any newborn, when expectant parents are asked about the preferred gender of their children, they often say they just want the baby to be healthy. Camille Geraldi is one woman you would never catch repeating that phrase. Beginning in 1986, Camille and her husband, Michael, adopted or became legal guardians to eighty-eight special-needs children. Eighty-eight! That's more than triple the active roster of a Major League Baseball team.

Camille always had a desire to help others who looked physically different. She was driven by both her oversized heart and her ability to empathize. She had been an overweight child, which resulted in constant mocking and scrutiny from others, even her own parents. Her father was especially critical of Camille, often berating her for her weight. He worked in women's fashion, a field known for its impossibly high standards for physical appearance. He considered Camille's weight to be a personal embarrassment, as though it reflected negatively on himself and his work. Camille understood what it was like to be noticed and ridiculed for her imperfections, and that led her to become more compassionate for others with physical differences.

Camille had a classmate in grade school who was mocked by other students because she dragged one foot behind her when she walked. Camille asked her mother what was wrong with the girl, and her mother explained that she had a tumor, which affected the way she walked and behaved. Camille began to understand that this girl could not help what made her different and that she had no choice but to deal with her physical limitations as best she could. Camille decided to befriend her and vowed never to judge a person on the basis of his or her appearance as her classmates had done.

When Camille was fifteen, she volunteered her time to work with mentally disabled children at Marian Center, a home and school in south Florida providing services for those with intellectual disabilities. Her father, a successful and wealthy businessman, donated large sums of money to this organization but was embarrassed by Camille's hands-on involvement. He happily publicized the fact that he supported causes financially, but he stopped short of offering any direct, personal assistance. It was as if such efforts were beneath him. Camille's father could not understand why Camille wanted to give so much of her time to the Marian Center. Camille, on the other hand, felt she was able to achieve so much more when she was in the field, dealing directly with the people who needed help. Even as a teenager, she understood the difference her actions could make in another person's life. Despite not having support from her parents, Camille continued to dedicate her spare time to helping those with disabilities.

Eventually, Camille turned her desire to help the disadvantaged into a career. Originally, she studied to become a special-education teacher, but she turned her focus to nursing when a friend of hers, reluctant to enter nursing school alone, asked Camille to join her. Thinking a nursing career would be rewarding, Camille agreed. It seemed like the perfect way to combine her need to pursue meaningful employment with her love of helping disabled children.

When she graduated from nursing school, Camille began a brief stint working with adult patients but quickly realized she preferred to work with children instead. She transferred to Variety Children's Hospital in Miami (now known as Nicklaus Children's Hospital), where she became a pediatric nurse in the intensive care unit. The intensive care unit at Variety was where Camille first met Michael, a new pediatric resident.

On the afternoon of July 4, 1973, four boys were involved in a near-drowning incident and rushed to Variety. They were admitted to the ICU and placed under strict observation. Camille, a seasoned ICU nurse at just twenty-four years old, worked with Michael and his four associates that day, teaching them how to talk to parents delicately about their children's conditions and prognoses. The five residents needed guidance in their new surroundings, and Camille took the reins in teaching them.

At around two in the morning, Michael worked his first on-call shift in the hospital and roamed the desolate halls of the ICU monitoring his sleeping patients. He was surrounded by silence except for the beeping of medical machines and the sweet singing voice of a woman he could not initially see. He followed that voice until he found Camille gently rocking a terminally ill baby in her arms, lulling her to sleep. When he asked why she was still at the hospital long after her shift had ended, Camille explained to Michael that the child was going to die that night and needed someone to be there for her. Oftentimes, children who weren't expected to live long or those who had severe disabilities would be abandoned in the hospital by their birth parents. This was one of those cases. Camille's compassion ensured these children would never die alone. Camille explained to Michael that she felt her calling in life was to care for children who needed it the most and that one day she wanted to open a home to provide a loving environment for the developmentally and physically disabled.

Michael, thirty years old at the time, was enamored of Camille's dedication to her young patients, a dedication that far surpassed that of anyone he had met before. His admiration for her only deepened over time. The two would eat lunch together outdoors with one of the sick children Camille would bring along. It was cumbersome lugging respirators and IV machines, but the reward far exceeded the inconvenience. Camille knew no one else would bring these children outside for fresh air, so she did it gladly. Michael fell for Camille's kindness, and he and Camille began dating.

Camille never imagined that Michael, a handsome, sought-after doctor, would choose her out of all the other nurses. At the time, Camille still carried excess weight and never really gave much thought to dating. But Michael noticed only the heart of gold that motivated Camille each day. In 1975, Michael and Camille married with the understanding that one day they would follow Camille's dream to open a home for children needing special assistance.

Michael's career as a pediatric doctor provided for an extraordinarily comfortable life. They did not want for anything. They lived in a large house with a pool and drove expensive cars.

In 1979, after the births of two daughters, Camille began to feel that her life was much too comfortable. Her family had become rooted in material possessions; her dream of creating a haven for special-needs children had fallen out of focus. When Camille and Michael were ready to expand their family, Camille insisted on adopting an infant who needed extra love and attention. She added their names to every adoption agency list she could find and explained they wanted a child with special needs because they were equipped to deal with the situation. Though both Michael and Camille worked in the medical field and were more than qualified to care for a child with a medical condition, they waited years for any news of a possible adoption. In

March 1986, Camille finally received word about a baby girl with Down syndrome in need of a loving home. Excitedly, Camille and Michael prepared to welcome this five-week-old baby into their hearts, a decision that would alter the course of the family's life forever.

Darlene, the new member of the Geraldi family, not only had Down syndrome, she was also deaf and showed characteristics of being autistic. Medical specialists called Darlene a "failure to thrive" baby, which meant she would never physically or mentally develop like other children. Camille refused to view her daughter that way; rather, she saw Darlene as simply another infant who brought her family joy. And that was enough for both Camille and Michael.

By 1988, Camille and Michael had added eight more adoptive children to their family, each of whom needed special care. Most had Down syndrome, but others had even more serious medical conditions, which required them to be under constant surveillance. Some had heart conditions, others required tracheostomy tubes or colostomy bags, and some were in persistent vegetative states. Camille and Michael made a home for the sickest of the sick, the children no one else wanted or for whom no one else could provide proper care. They became known as the couple to call when someone had a child they could not (or did not want to) care for. Local hospitals contacted Camille whenever parents abandoned their sick newborns. Celebrities approached Camille when they did not want to bother with an imperfect child. And some families were given the Geraldis' names when they needed short-term relief known as respite care.

"To this day, we are called from well-known celebrities and athletes and people all over the world, and we've always promised them that we would never expose them or their child to the media," Camille says. "Many news reporters would call, searching for that famous child."

Camille and Michael went into each situation not knowing what they would find. Sometimes parents desperately wanted to keep their children but did not have the means to care for them, so they opted to keep in close contact with the Geraldis to learn of their children's progress. Other times, the birth parents chose to deal with their children callously and indifferently, handing them over to the Geraldis at the airport completely naked. Even more outrageous: On about fifteen different occasions, a baby was left on the Geraldis' doorstep without so much as a note. Camille could never turn those babies away. Some parents knew very little about Down syndrome and would bring their infants to see Michael at his pediatric practice. There, Michael would lay out the facts of the syndrome and what life would be like for the parents and child. He offered all the information he could and allowed the parents to make an informed decision on whether they thought they could care for the child. If they could not, he suggested finding a good group home that cared for special-needs children, and on occasion he offered his own home as a solution.

Of course, there were moments when the Geraldis had their doubts about adding more children to their household. In the early stages, the Geraldis adopted only girls. They decided it would be best for the family to have only one gender as the children grew to be adolescents. However, when a hospital contacted Camille to ask if she was interested in adopting the son of a South American model, she said yes after only a brief moment of hesitation. She knew this little boy with Down syndrome needed to be loved just as much as anyone else. While Camille understood that some of the birth parents she encountered could not afford to care for a child with medical issues, this boy's parents were wealthy and had the means to raise him. Their disdain for his condition made Camille want to adopt him even more.

By 1997, the Geraldis had adopted and cared for forty-one children with disabilities, most with Down syndrome or other cognitive development issues. Although she hired ten full-time employees to help care for these children, Camille was still very much a hands-on mother. She slept very little at night, waking to feed the babies, check on the children who had trouble breathing on their own, and change colostomy bags. She found joy in the little moments of her day, such as when babies born with half a brain smiled at her and when the older children helped care for their younger siblings. To her, these children made her home and her life extraordinary.

One person also believed Camille herself to be extraordinary: President George H.W. Bush. In 1991, he named

Camille one of the nation's "Points of Light," which is also the name of the foundation he formed in 1990 to recognize organizations and individuals who stood at the forefront of service. The honor bestowed on Camille led to media attention for the Geraldis, and they were featured on shows such as *60 Minutes* and *The 700 Club*. The publicity allowed Michael and Camille to grow their own foundation, known at the time as "Up with Downs," which allowed for donations to aid in the family's skyrocketing cost of living.

"Because I served the Lord, I never looked for recognition," Camille says. "All I ever ask is that people pray for my health, because without health, you have nothing. All I ever wanted was to be there for my children."

Prior to starting the foundation, Michael's salary as a doctor financed Camille's passion for adopting and caring for special-needs children. As the number of Geraldi children grew, so did their medical expenses, grocery bills, and staffing needs. In her book, *Camille's Children: Thirty-One Miracles and Counting*, Camille outlines the family's monthly living expenses in the early 1990s: $1,800 for electricity, $2,500 for groceries, $1,200 for diapers, $800 for clothes, and $8,600 for medical care. That was in addition to the $22,000 the foundation cost per month to operate. Those costs included staff salaries, insurance premiums, car payments, gas, mortgages, and more. The Geraldis also spent between $6,000 and $10,000 in adoption fees whenever a new child entered the family.

The Geraldi house grew to a three-structure compound in the same South Florida neighborhood in which the Geraldis had always lived. Michael and Camille owned the original house, the foundation owned the second house, and they rented the third house. The homes sat adjacent to one another and shared one expansive backyard. Each house had a different purpose. One served as the foundation's office space and was also where the children were dressed and fed; they all slept in the second house, and the last house was used for clerical work.

Camille ran a tight ship in her compound. She loved every child who entered her home, and she expected a lot from each of them. Camille saw potential in every child, even if the biological parents did not. Because of that, each child went to public school at the appropriate age and was placed in a special-education program. If a child was too sick to physically attend school, Camille made sure he or she learned through a homeschool program.

Camille's dedication to her children enriched their lives. The attention and care she and her staff gave allowed the children to flourish. She did not coddle them or allow their disabilities to be viewed as setbacks. She was strict with her children, and her sternness taught the children how to behave and how to obey rules.

Camille kept an organized home, which allowed it to run smoothly. The staff kept to schedules, and the children had routines. If the children learned how to be organized, how to exercise proper hygiene, and how to pay attention, they would better fit into society as adults. Everything Camille did for her children was to teach them how to live full, independent lives and become functioning members of society, even if they would never achieve the mental maturity of typical adults.

Every child had a chart with twenty individually tailored goals varying from physical, mental, and social skills. Camille and her staff met monthly to discuss the progress the children were making, and they placed special emphasis on speech, cognition, and motor skills. Camille was more than just a mother to these children. She gave them a home when everyone else abandoned them, and she loved them when no one else dared. She dedicated her time to making sure each child reached his or her potential.

"I wanted them to be accepted and never shunned," Camille says. "Unfortunately, most handicapped adults have a very hard time fitting into society. They were my dream and lifelong dedication."

Because Camille was an incredibly hands-on mother and the head of the Up with Downs Foundation, she rarely had time for herself. Raising an ever-growing number of children with disabilities was laborious. Camille constantly had to be on duty as she monitored the children with troubled breathing, heart conditions, and feeding tubes. And she had to deal with the emotional stress of being a parent to children who required multiple surgeries. She stood at the hospital bedside of her children as a mother, not as a nurse, which carried a much different weight. Camille also dealt with incredible loss, including the death of children too sick to heal from their illnesses, as well as reversed adoptions when parents became capable of caring for their biological offspring.

Another of the struggles Camille faced continually had to do with the misperceptions some people had about her motivations. Many people did not believe Camille had only good intentions for adopting as many children as she did. They assumed she was driven by financial greed. Camille assured her naysayers there was no financial gain in being a mother and caretaker to as many developmentally disabled children as she had. More importantly, there was no ulterior motive to her kindness. In fact, her life was made much more difficult because of her open heart. One time, one of her children wore the same shirt to school two days in a row. The teacher noticed and asked Camille not to let this happen again. Camille had to explain that because she had such an expansive family, they often bought clothes in bulk and the children would share. Unintentionally, a child might wear an identical shirt two days in a row if it ended up in his or her closet after the laundry was done, but it was never the same shirt from the previous day. The teacher turned this incident over to the state because she felt that each child should have his or her own wardrobe and closet. The state came to the home to perform a welfare check on the family and was satisfied when Camille demonstrated that each child had his or her own section of a massive closet.

Another challenge Camille faced was the amount of attention she and her family attracted wherever they went. Some people recognized them from the specials on television, while others just gawked at them because of their appearance. There were times when Camille felt her heart shatter as a result of callous behavior exhibited by others. Once, she had been at a mall in Boca Raton, and a stranger approached her. Camille was carrying one of her babies and the woman lifted the corner of the blanket to see the child's face. Satisfied to see the child had Down syndrome, she lowered the blanket, turned to walk away, and said coldly to Camille, "I thought you were the one."

Camille noticed such behavior every place she went; the condescending tone that the salespeople at a store would use with her, the pointing and laughing she saw from teenagers out of the corner of her eye, and the deliberate manner in which many people avoided her family in public. It was in these moments that Camille wanted to retreat with her kids and keep them safe at home, keep them out of the critical public eye, keep them innocent and unaware of the label society had put on them. But Camille also realized that no one learned how to succeed in life by being shielded from adversity, so she proudly let her children be exactly who they were, whether at home or in public.

Camille's work and family created conflicts with some neighbors. As the Geraldis' foundation grew, the residents of their neighborhood became resistant to its good deeds. They felt the neighborhood was being overrun by the developmentally disabled and that this lowered their property values. The Geraldis became targets. They received numerous threatening phone calls, and their property was vandalized. Someone poured acid on a staffer's car and then broke all the car windows. The house was egged many times. Neighbors told the Geraldis to move. Michael hired a couple bodyguards to protect his family and staff, but both Michael and Camille understood the environment was becoming much too hostile to remain there.

In 1992, the Geraldis began to move their family to a twenty-five-acre property in North Carolina in hopes of providing the children with a safer, more accepting life. They kept the homes in Florida because not all the children were able to leave. Some were just too sick and needed constant medical attention that was not available at their location in North Carolina. Michael still had his pediatric practice in Miami, so he stayed behind to watch over those children while Camille oversaw the rest of the family in North Carolina.

The community in North Carolina was much more welcoming and proved to be the change Camille needed for her family. The Geraldis grew and canned their own fruits and vegetables, raised horses, dogs, and chickens, and lived without fear of persecution. But of course, Camille did not want to desert Michael and her other children in Florida. She was still the matriarch of the unique family. Camille decided to split her time between the two homes by spending twenty days a month in North Carolina and ten in Florida. The children who stayed in Florida were still Camille's children, and they needed her love and attention, too.

As the years passed and the children grew older, money became a problem for the Geraldis. People stopped donating to the foundation because, as Camille recounted, "Once children with Down syndrome become adults, people stop thinking they're cute. Society has a tendency to focus on the needs of children, but what happens when they age?" Michael had hoped to eventually move to North Carolina to be with Camille, but as donations to the foundation dwindled, Michael knew his salary kept the family and foundation afloat. It would be too difficult to start a new practice from scratch in a different state, so Michael and Camille lived apart until Michael passed away from cancer in 2016.

Today, Camille lives in Georgia (their North Carolina home burned down after a lightning strike in 2011) with the remaining three foundation staff members and the twenty-five children still in her care, most of whom are now adults. The foundation, now known as the Possible Dream Foundation, no longer accepts new children. Camille is sixty-nine years old and has decided to concentrate on the quality of life of those children who live with her as well as her own well-being, something she promised Michael before he died. She knows she needs to be there for her family, which she can't do if she overextends herself.

Even though Camille has slowed down, the fruits of her labor are witnessed daily. Her children lead fulfilling lives. The foundation has a center where the children train dogs to be both police canines and personal companions. The children help with chores around the house, such as picking fruits and vegetables from the garden and folding laundry, and they work on crafts in their spare time to stay active and motivated. Camille's insistence on activity and routine, beginning in childhood, has allowed her children to become higher-functioning adults, which is one of the greatest rewards she could receive for dedicating her entire life to a benevolent cause. Her children do not live completely on their own, but Camille's help has taught them to be more than just a label society has placed on them.

There have been moments when Camille has wondered what her life would have been like had she and Michael not chosen to adopt children and start the foundation. They would have spent a lot more time alone together, lived life the way typical married couples do, and gone on vacations together, something they never had the chance to do in all their years of marriage. But Camille does not regret how her life turned out. She is surrounded by more love than she ever imagined.

Camille has lived an extraordinary life. She changed the lives of countless children who otherwise might never have been given the chance to survive, let alone live an ordinary life. Camille regards her work as a vocation.

"It was never a choice for me to care for the children no one else wanted; it was just something I always felt called to do," she explains.

In the end, she adopted thirty-one of the eighty-eight children in her care, but all eighty-eight consider her to be their mother. And she is. She is the woman who showed them love, compassion, and acceptance when others would not. She is the one who invested her time, money, and heart into ensuring they reached their full potential. Camille Geraldi might be only one woman in this world, but she is the one woman who changed the world for eighty-eight children.

....

If you'd like to support Camille's work, please visit the Possible Dream Foundation at possibledream.org.

Odalys

Imagine a land rich with sugar cane and lush, tropical vegetation, an island teeming with coastal villages framed by endless miles of azure waters. To romantics and dreamers, such descriptions conjure up visions of paradise on earth. But as is often the case, there is more to this apparent utopia than meets the eye. Imagine that same exotic island to be home to the kind of hedonistic pleasures that tantalize even the most innocent of minds, an environment that tempts and beckons all kinds of pleasure seekers, from gamblers to golfers and everyone in between.

This was Cuba, or at least the way most people thought of Cuba, in the 1920s, decades before the revolution. It was a country where the privileged lifestyle of the elite collided with the more relaxed, bohemian lifestyle of the masses. The two groups coexisted well enough for a time, but that would all change in the decades that followed.

As airfare from the United States dropped in price after World War II, Havana saw an increase in tourism. People were drawn to the city by its numerous casinos and nightclubs, its carefree environment, and its reputation as a mecca for adult entertainment. By the 1950s, Havana's secret was out; it was no longer a destination favored only by the wealthy—celebrities such as Ernest Hemingway and Ava Gardner. The price of all-inclusive travel packages to the island had become so affordable that even Americans with modest incomes could immerse themselves in Havana's lifestyle. But that lifestyle was not always appreciated by the local residents, especially when their own fortunes took a turn for the worse.

During the 1950s, Cuba experienced an economic downturn. Tourist-driven Havana did not feel the effects of that decline very much, but residents in outlying areas did. Soon, many of those people became restless and increasingly intolerant of activities in the capital city. They viewed much of the behavior exhibited by people in Havana as inappropriate, excessive, and, at times, immoral.

Beyond the city limits of Havana, a revolution percolated. In 1959, that revolution toppled the government, and Cuba fell into the hands of Fidel Castro, who established a Communist dictatorship on the island. Almost instantly, Cuba became a land of repression and persecution. Much of the country's development that had been initiated during the prior administration came to a standstill. More importantly, the comfortable lifestyle that many Cuban people enjoyed before the revolution was gone, only to be replaced by a life of poverty, anarchy, and fear.

Odalys Reyna was born in the early years of Castro's Cuba in 1961. In 1967, her family made the difficult decision to flee their homeland in the hopes of finding a better life in the United States. Odalys's parents, Neticia and Reginaldo, applied for the family to migrate from Cuba on a "Freedom Flight," which was a collaboration between the United States and Cuban governments to provide a safe, orderly means of emigration for people seeking to leave the island nation. Around this time, there were roughly two million Cubans wishing to leave, though only about half had submitted applications. Shortly after Odalys's family had applied for exit visas, they were labeled "enemies of the state." Immediately thereafter, the government froze all their assets. Subsequently, Odalys's father lost his job and in 1968 was sent to work in a labor camp. There he was required to earn his freedom to leave Cuba by performing hard labor, thus assuring the Cuban government he would be putting something back into the system before being allowed to leave the country. While in the camp, Reginaldo worked in the fields from dawn to dusk every day and slept in a tent. He was allowed to visit home only once a month, so Neticia, Odalys, and her brother, Carlos, visited Reginaldo at the labor camp once a week. During those visits, they brought food and clean clothes, as well as a hope that their patriarch would not have to endure life in a camp much longer.

Odalys reflects on that time: "I was around six when my father first went to the labor camp. I didn't grasp why he was gone, and my parents did a great job of shielding me from that. I missed him and looked forward to his monthly visits home. This homecoming was an anticipation much like a military family would have when their loved one came home on leave. It became a way of life for us. It was my normal."

With the family's assets frozen, Neticia needed to find a way to provide for her son and young daughter. She didn't know when they would receive the telegram notifying the family of their approval to leave Cuba, but she could not sit back and watch her children starve. Though she technically was not allowed to earn money at the time, she did what was necessary for their survival. She secretly (and illegally) continued to work in her trade as a seamstress. Odalys grew up fairly poor, but she didn't mind. The little her mother could contribute to the family was sufficient.

Every day, Odalys and her family waited for the news that they had been granted leave from Cuba, but every day they continued to be disappointed. As time passed and their salvation did not come, it seemed as though tiny pieces of their hearts were being broken away. Worse, they felt time was running out for them to make their escape. In Cuba at the time, when any able-bodied boy turned fifteen, he would not be permitted to leave the country again until he turned twenty-seven. Males between the ages of fifteen and twenty-seven were ideal for service in the military. In light of that, Odalys's family had decided that if they did not receive approval to leave Cuba by the time Carlos turned fifteen, they would all remain there together. Their parents refused to leave anyone behind to suffer alone at the hands of Communism.

When Carlos turned fourteen, his parents considered another route that would buy slightly more time for the family in their quest to reach America. Teenage boys (under fifteen) could apply to be sent to Spain through an application process similar to the "Freedom Flights." Though this would mean breaking up their family for a short while, Odalys's parents saw this as a viable last resort. If they wanted to leave the island at all, their first mission had to be to save Carlos. Ignoring the deep heartache she felt for even considering this option, Neticia applied to send her son alone to a foreign country—the only option available to her, ironically, to keep her family together. As Odalys reflects on her parents' decision now, being a mother herself, she can only imagine how difficult it must have been to send Carlos away. But when faced with that decision, Odalys's parents did so with conviction. There was no room for doubt in a time of such turmoil.

As the months crept closer to Carlos's fifteenth birthday and the family still had not heard about his acceptance to emigrate to Spain, Neticia took matters into her own hands. Time was of the essence. She decided to make the five-hour drive to Havana in order to speak directly to a high-ranking official about her son's departure. Not knowing what the man looked like, Neticia stalked the appropriate government building for a week, observing every detail of who came and went. She watched and waited patiently before she was able to make her move.

Finally, after a week of diligent surveillance, Neticia discovered who the appropriate immigration officer was and deftly worked her way into his assistant's office. After listening to her plea for help, the assistant told Neticia she should return home. At the same time, she promised to help speed up the process for Carlos to receive his visa to travel to Spain, a promise that did not come to fruition.

Despite the visit to Havana, as of early April, Neticia still had not received any word on Carlos's departure date. By that time, Odalys's parents knew something had to be done quickly. Carlos would turn fifteen in two short weeks and the family would be trapped in Cuba indefinitely if he could not get out before then. Odalys was eight years old and understood well enough that her family life was in turmoil; she just didn't know why. She was too young to fully grasp the severity of the situation or what it would mean to grow up under the yoke of Communism. All she knew was that the family needed to escape for some reason.

With time now becoming a critical factor, Reginaldo risked severe punishment and snuck out of his labor camp to help his wife devise a plan. They decided it would be best if Neticia again attempted to speak with someone in Havana, this time someone higher up in the bureaucracy. Learning who that individual was before she left, Neticia made the trek back to Havana determined to meet with the second-highest emigration officer on staff. Again, she watched and waited, observing every move of the guards until the opportune moment arrived when she could slip into the man's office. With the utmost stealth, Neticia slipped into the office of this official and made a desperate plea for assistance. By the grace of God, as she firmly believes, he agreed to send Carlos a telegram containing his departure information within the week. Neticia did not truly understand why the government official assisted her; perhaps he took pity on her after listening to her sad story, or perhaps he was impressed by her courage. Either way, when Neticia learned that another desperate mother tried the same maneuver the following week and was summarily executed, she understood how fortunate she was. Neticia drove back to Havana with a renewed sense of hope that her family still had a chance for a better life off the island.

"It wasn't until I was in my teens that I understood the full extent of what my mother had done," Odalys explains. "I was only eight at the time, so I just knew that my mom had to go talk to an emigration officer about my brother's paperwork. It was very matter-of-fact. My parents shielded me from the reality and severity of the situation. As I got older, I realized the risk my mom took and how amazing she was for doing it."

On April 14, 1970, Carlos received the telegram authorizing him to emigrate to Spain. According to the paperwork, he was to leave Cuba on April 16, a mere four days before his fifteenth birthday. When that date arrived, Odalys and her parents drove Carlos to the airport to say their final goodbyes. Fear and uncertainty hung in the air. No one knew whether the rest of the family would make it to the United States, and if they did, when that might be. It could still be years from now—maybe never. And even if they made it, Carlos would still need to travel from Spain to Miami to be with them. In spite of all the uncertainty, the underlying feeling for every member of Odalys's family was relief. At least now Carlos would be guaranteed a taste of freedom when he arrived in Spain.

After the family said their tearful farewells, they watched Carlos walk through the doors of the glass structure known as the fishbowl. This was a room in the middle of the airport where government officials scrutinized the documents and possessions of anyone leaving. One misstep during the interrogation process, and Carlos's departure to Madrid would be denied. They waited in silence with pounding hearts and knotted stomachs until finally Carlos turned to them, waved, and walked deeper into the airport. He was on his way to freedom.

Odalys and her parents walked toward the window to watch Carlos's plane take off. As they waited, her mother dropped to her knees, overcome by emotion. Odalys heard her mother say, "I may never see him again, but God protect him." Having made a promise to stop smoking cigars if his son was able to flee Cuba, Odalys's father took two Cuban cigars from the breast pocket of his button-up shirt and gave them to a man standing next to him. "Here," he said, "I don't smoke anymore." Reginaldo had been a chain smoker for over twenty years, but on that day, he gave up his vice permanently without hesitation.

After Carlos's plane departed, the family returned to their hotel room in Havana for the evening. Late at night, they received a phone call, which Reginaldo answered in the hotel lobby. When he returned to the room, he did not tell the family the nature of the call, because it would have upset everyone. Later, however, when the news was no longer an issue, he revealed that Carlos's plane had turned around because of mechanical issues. At the time, the airline did not know how quickly the repairs could be made, but there was a real possibility the flight would not leave for another few days. With Carlos turning fifteen on April 20, that meant he would not be able to leave Cuba. Fortunately, however, mechanics were able to fix the problem that night and the plane took off for Spain once again with Carlos on board.

With Odalys's brother now in Spain and being cared for by a charity organization that aided exiled teenagers, Odalys's family resumed their normal lives. Neticia continued to sew in secrecy, and Reginaldo returned to the labor camp where his escape had earned him three months in solitary confinement.

On September 10, 1970, the family received their own telegram from the Cuban government authorizing their departure to Miami. The telegram was hand-delivered by Cuban militiamen, who entered the family's home and took an inventory of all their possessions. When the family left Cuba, they would not be permitted to take any belongings with them except the clothing they wore plus one extra set of clothing. If they attempted to remove any other items from the home, the family would be punished. One of the officers reached for the doll Odalys held through the entire ordeal and ripped it from her. "You can't take this," he gruffly declared. Odalys broke into hysterics, and surprisingly, the officer thrust the doll back into her arms.

The officers continued ransacking the house looking for anything and everything the family could be hiding. Eventually, they relented and gave up their search. At last, Odalys's family was free to move onto their new lives.

"At eight years old, I was extremely sad to be leaving Cuba," Odalys says. "I remember saying goodbye to all of the family that final day. Everyone was crying and saying, 'Oh, we'll see you soon.' I didn't understand why everyone was so emotional when we would be seeing each other again soon. Of course, that wasn't the case. Eventually, some aunts and uncles visited us briefly in America, but there are some family members I never saw again, like my paternal grandmother. We've never been back to Cuba, and as long as it's a Communist country, we won't step foot on the island. It would be such a dishonor to the sacrifices my parents made in order to get us to America."

As they drove past their home one final time, they reflected on their lives in Cuba. Nearly three years had passed since they submitted their "Freedom Flight" application. They had been a broken family for all that time. Reginaldo stayed in the forced work camp for the entire thirty-month waiting period, and Carlos was forced to endure juvenile camp until the time of his departure to Spain. Through all those years, the family never lost hope. They explored every option and knew one day they would leave Cuba for a better life in the United States. And though they knew their family would not be whole in Miami when they arrived there, they were confident that Carlos would join them in due time. On September 16, five months to the day after her brother left for Spain, Odalys, her parents, and her maternal grand-mother boarded the plane for Miami.

The family arrived in Miami without any possessions or money, and they didn't speak English. But while they were destitute, they were not hopeless. They knew that if they had stayed in Cuba, not only would they have faced a life of poverty and hopelessness, they would have faced a perse-cution and repression as well. Odalys's family arrived in America with nothing, but they understood that was simply the beginning of a new life in a strange country, one that would have to be built from the ground up. The prospect of freedom overshadowed any trepidation they felt.

After they got off the plane, Odalys and her family maneu-vered through the airport terminal uncertain of what was ahead. Odalys spotted a vending machine that dispensed ice cream sandwiches. She begged her father to buy one for her, but he did not have any money. With a broken-hearted Odalys in tow, the family continued on their way to meet up with members from the Liberty House, a charitable organization in Miami. This organization greeted all of the Cuban immigrants at the airport and aided their assimilation into the new country.

While still at the airport, Reginaldo saw an old friend he knew from Cuba. This friend handed him ten dollars to help the family get started in America, a gesture Odalys still remembers vividly.

"The first thing my father bought using that money was an ice cream sandwich from the vending machine," she says. "That provided me with my first taste of the 'American Dream.'"

For their first night in the United States, Odalys and her family stayed at Liberty House. The following day, they moved into a small efficiency apartment with a relative and her son who previously had come from Cuba. That December, Carlos flew over from Spain and joined the family in Florida. By then, they had moved into a one-bedroom apartment. They feasted on hot dogs and bologna sandwiches and watched every penny that came into and left their pockets.

"I thought America was great!" Odalys remembers. "It wasn't always easy, but that didn't matter to me. My family was together. In some ways, it was very eye-opening. The Communist lifestyle was all I knew at that point in my life.

Eating cornmeal and eggs for lunch was my normal. I didn't know there was steak in the world. The same goes for toy stores. In Cuba, children played with paper dolls and played hopscotch. When I walked into a toy store for the first time, my jaw dropped.

"I turned nine years old the week after we arrived in the United States, and my older cousin asked me what I wanted for my birthday. I had never been asked that before. I didn't know what to say. I didn't even know what toys were available to me. Then she asked me if I wanted a bicycle and I said yes. So for my ninth birthday, I received my very first bicycle with training wheels because I didn't know how to ride."

Of course, not all aspects of assimilating to life in the United States were easy, as Odalys recalls: "I didn't speak any English, so school was very tough at first. It was like gibberish to me. The only classes I passed that first year were math classes. I got A's in those because I was actually ahead in math when I came to America. It took me about a year and a half to learn English. We weren't allowed to watch Spanish television at home, so I watched a lot of cartoons in English. The language barrier was the roughest in the beginning, but I wasn't shy about trying to speak my new language or making mistakes. That was the start of my new life."

Reginaldo worked at various factory jobs but did not find anything permanent in Florida. One day, he was offered a full-time job at a window factory in Southern California. The family of five uprooted again and trekked across the country for another fresh start. Again, they crammed into a one-bedroom apartment, with Odalys's parents sleeping in the bedroom and Odalys and her grandma sleeping on the L-shaped sectional in the living room. A partition was set up off to the side of the living room to provide teenage Carlos with a bit of privacy. The situation wasn't ideal, but they made it work and knew it wouldn't last forever.

The family found success in California. While Reginaldo worked in the factory, Odalys's mother began her own sewing company. Between the ages of ten and twelve, every day after school Odalys came home, ate a snack, and then joined her mother in her shop. She handled the menial tasks, such as sewing buttons. After her father came home from work, they ate dinner as a family and then Odalys and her mother resumed their work at the sewing shop until about ten at night. The fruits of all this hard work allowed the family to move out of their tiny apartment and buy their own house. Reginaldo worked at that same window factory until his retirement.

"I realized the importance in us moving to the United States once my brother arrived from Spain," Odalys shares. "I saw how hard my parents had worked to get us here. Then we moved to California and our lives started coming together. My parents were really good about always telling my brother and me, 'We came here so that you could be anything you want to be and achieve anything you want to achieve, but right now we have to work hard to get there.'

Once I matured and reached my teenage years, everything clicked. I was in awe of everything my parents did for us to have a life full of opportunities."

Odalys reflects on her childhood with gratitude and admiration for her parents. They made the difficult decision to uproot their lives, to send their teenage son to a foreign country alone, and to start a fresh life in a new country without a penny to their names. Odalys knows it took them massive amounts of courage and strength to risk everything for a chance at freedom.

Odalys considers her mother to be one of her greatest inspirations. "My mom was always so strong; she was a go-getter. Nothing was impossible. She always told me, 'Don't ever think you can't do something.' That was instilled in me. I know I can achieve anything that I set my mind to as long as I work hard. My mom had an elementary-school education, but that never prevented her from going after what she wanted."

What Odalys originally wanted was to become a nurse. Though she never went to college because her family could not afford it, she did go to school to become a medical assistant. For a year, she worked in a doctor's office before deciding she wanted to continue her education with some night courses.

"I was twenty years old taking a business law course, and on the first night we went around the room introducing ourselves," Odalys recalls. "There was a man who said he worked for employee relations at the Walt Disney Company, and I was in awe wondering what it must be like to work for Disney. Over the next couple of classes on our breaks, I started chatting with him. We talked about what I was doing with my life and how I was continuing my education. He said how he loved to see hardworking people go after their goals and if I ever needed a job, I should apply at Disney and put his name down. I had been questioning my job as a medical assistant, and I was also dating the man who later became my husband. I knew when I started a family I didn't want to work nights and weekends, which I would have to do as a nurse. Out of the blue, I decided to apply at Disney. When I interviewed for a position in the merchandise office, they hired me on the spot. I've been with the company ever since—about thirty-six years."

Odalys lives each day believing hard work and determination should never be wasted. And she takes nothing for granted. She understands just how lucky she is to live in a free nation. She feels blessed for every single opportunity she has been granted and refuses to waste a second of her time on earth.

"I am the spitting image of my parents when it comes to drive and determination," Odalys says. "It irks me when I hear people complain how hard their lives are. Yes, life can be hard, but think of all the opportunities we have here in the United States. It's still the best country in the world. People still want to come here, and there's a reason for that."

The many people who know Odalys and have heard her remarkable story of immigrating to America will say she inspires them to be courageous and to never quit. Even in her darkest days, Odalys chooses to stay strong, something she learned from her parents. In 2009, her son was killed in a car accident. No mother wants to outlive her child; Odalys is no exception. And while she did grieve for her unimaginable loss, she also decided she would not let his death overshadow his life.

"After my son's death, people asked me how I moved on," she says. "What other option did I have? The different situations throughout my life taught me to roll up my sleeves and face whatever was thrown at me. I could curl into a fetal position, but what good would that do?"

Odalys admits that there are days when she just wants to throw the covers over her head and hide from the world, but she doesn't. Instead, she chooses to find strength. She says, "People have told me that I am so strong, but strength is a choice. You can choose to be strong or you can choose to buckle. Being anything other than strong was never an option for me."

Odalys lives her life just as her parents did: with unwavering strength and courage.

Today, the dress Odalys wore on her journey to the United States hangs in one of the closets in her home. The doll she brought with her sits on a shelf in a bedroom. Both symbolize not only the past she left behind but also the rewards of freedom. To Odalys, these items remind her how the decisions we make throughout our lives shape our future. She is a fighter and a pillar of strength. You will never see her give up; quitting is not something she knows how to do.

"The role models I had were such a big influence in my life. Not just my parents, but everyone who surrounded me. They were all go-getters," Odalys says. "Now, I try to be a good role model for other people by staying positive. Yes, sometimes it is hard to do, but I try to look for the good in everything. I take everything bad that's happened in my life and turn it into a positive, not just for me, but for other people. The other option is to be bitter and angry, but what good is that going to do for me or others? My son did more in his twenty-one years on earth than most people do in their lifetime. I refuse to let the one day he died be the focus of his life. I do a lot of service work with the homeless because my son was passionate about that. And I reach out to other mothers who have lost children, because I am a believer in giving back. If I can help someone by sharing my experiences, I will."

One September day in 1970, an eight-year-old girl boarded a plane destined for an unknown life. What she found when she arrived was a land of infinite opportunities made possible by hope, hard work, and fortitude—three traits Odalys Reyna will never abandon.

"Over the years, I learned that life is not fair, but you keep moving forward one day at a time," she says. "Life is so precious and fragile. We learn so many lessons throughout our lives, and after a while they all start accumulating into who we become. Hard work and family values were two of the greatest lessons ever instilled in me. I feel a great sense of accomplishment when I see my daughter start to value the same things as I do, as my parents do. It's like watching everything come full circle.

"To me, the American Dream is ongoing. It hasn't always been easy; there were a lot of sacrifices along the way. And though life in the United States may be full of hard work, the beauty is that you get to enjoy the fruits of your labor. I always count my blessings and think how my parents' sacrifices were totally worth it. Their sacrifices led me to the amazing life that I have now."

If you'd like to support an organization close to Odalys's heart, please visit Second Harvest Food Bank of Central Florida at feedhopenow.org.

Danielle

On the afternoon of December 5, 2005, Danielle McCarthy walked into the theme park where she worked, thinking her shift at the Christmas event that day would be no different than the one prior. Little did she know a fluke accident on the job would change her life, setting her on a journey that involved medical emergencies, heartbreak and betrayal, and a tumor named Loretta that ultimately empowered Danielle to find her strength and her voice.

When Danielle arrived at work, she clocked in and headed straight to the outdoor theater where the Christmas performances were held. She greeted the guests who had begun to line up for the first performance, and as she moved down the line, she adjusted the stanchions that marked where the guests would stand as they waited. But one stanchion, placed into the ground improperly, didn't budge as Danielle attempted to lift it. Her left thumb became tangled in the eye, the loop where the rope snaked through, and twisted into an unnatural position. As Danielle freed it from the eye, her thumb immediately started to swell and turn purple. She fell to the ground, screaming in pain. One of the guests ran to get a cup of ice as Danielle lay in agony.

Despite the pain, Danielle rose from the ground to continue to work. She applied the ice to her thumb, which offered some relief, and went about her duties.

"Today, I realize the pain and agony I endured that day was nothing compared to the journey I was about to embark on," Danielle says. "I thought I knew the concept of pain. I was sadly mistaken."

It did not take long for Danielle's injury to show itself, and her manager directed her to the health services office on the premises.

The nurse at health services did not think the injury was serious. She placed Danielle's wrist in a plastic cast and told her to come back in two weeks. Over those two weeks, the pain only worsened. Danielle went back to health services for her follow-up and told the nurse she was still in excruciating pain, but the nurse assured Danielle it would simply be a matter of time before the thumb healed.

Because Danielle was injured on the job, the only medical care she received for her injury to that point was through her employer's health services. Because her injury fell under workers' compensation coverage, Danielle had to receive a referral from the health services office in order to see any doctors outside of their practice. Because they had a few doctors of their own, they refused to refer her elsewhere.

Over the next several months, Danielle's condition deteriorated so badly that her thumb was permanently folded across the palm of her hand, as if she were making the number four sign. Finally, the nurse authorized Danielle to visit an outside specialist.

Beginning in March 2006, she visited numerous specialists and tried various treatments. It was a nonstop whirlwind of visits, procedures, and therapies that lasted about four years. Danielle tried everything possible, including trigger-finger release, in which a tendon was cut to try to give the thumb a wider range of motion. She had nerve blocks inserted under her arm, in her neck, and in her spine to try to lessen her pain. Doctors also inserted a catheter into Danielle's arm to inject pain medication, something Danielle required on a daily basis. She attempted Botox injections in hopes they would calm the muscle spasms in her thumb. She even tried biofeedback therapy in an attempt to regain normal function of her hand by sparking brain communication. When that didn't work, Danielle kept searching for answers. She was beginning to lose the feeling in her thumb.

Eventually Danielle made an appointment with the Mayo Clinic in Jacksonville, Florida. There, she underwent multiple nerve tests, which involved jabbing her arm with a needle and shocking her at the same time.

Though the tests were torturous for Danielle, they provided an answer. Danielle was diagnosed with Reflex Sympathetic Dystrophy (RSD), a rare disorder that affects the nerves after tissue damage caused by trauma. Essentially Danielle's brain stopped communicating to her hand because she was in so much pain for such a long period of time that her brain needed to protect itself from continued discomfort. It cut off nerve signals, blood supply, and oxygen so Danielle would not feel pain. Her left hand was basically dying because it wasn't receiving any communication from her brain. And because the trauma had lasted for four years, the brain would not fuse the connection again.

As soon as Danielle returned to Orlando, she began searching for a hand surgeon to help her in the next step of her journey. She was referred to Dr. Geoff Black, who performed surgery to give Danielle's hand more mobility. Still, Danielle did not gain full range of motion after the surgery. Her hand remained unusable and arthritic-looking, and Dr. Black deemed Danielle's hand disabled.

Despite the disability, Danielle managed to function well during the next few years and found employment with an architectural firm that worked extensively with nearby Central Florida hospitals. She also rekindled a relationship with her ex-boyfriend, and within a year, they started living together. Though Danielle still struggled with the use of her left hand, life seemed to be less worrisome. Unfortunately, it did not take long for things to change.

In May 2015, Danielle underwent a tonsillectomy, a surgery she should have had when she was a child. Because she endured so many tests and procedures for her hand, her body had become intolerant to pain medicine. After her tonsils were removed, nurses had to give Danielle more medication than usual so she could feel any effects. It ended up being too high a dosage for Danielle, and she couldn't function properly for three months. She was out of work and lost a significant amount of weight.

Eventually, Danielle was able to resume her regular life, but she never felt quite the same as before her tonsil surgery. She couldn't pinpoint why. She developed earaches and sore throats, which she thought would have stopped after the surgery. Her left hand also started bothering her again.

In September 2015, Danielle flew to Houston to be with her grandfather, who was gravely ill. While there, she suffered from her first panic attack. Between rapid, shallow breaths and heavy sobs, she told her mom, "Something's not right. Something's not right. I don't know what it is, but I just don't feel right. Something's not normal."

Danielle couldn't figure out if something in her relationship with her boyfriend was wrong, or if it was health-related. She couldn't describe how or what she felt, or even why she felt it, but she knew something was amiss.

Knowing she needed to figure out what was going on with her body, Danielle looked first to the place where she knew she had an issue—her left thumb. She had been experiencing spasms in her thumb even though the muscle controlling it had been removed five years earlier. A few days before Thanksgiving in 2015, Danielle found herself back in Dr. Black's office searching for answers about her hand. Dr. Black took one look and knew the spasms weren't normal. He ordered five MRIs to be done on Danielle's hand and brain. The testing lasted nearly six hours and left Danielle physically drained.

The Monday after Thanksgiving, Danielle got her test results. A knot formed in the pit of her stomach as she expected some type of bad news. When Dr. Black came into the room, he greeted Danielle with a somber, "How are you?" This didn't fit his usual personality. Something must have been wrong.

Dr. Black had always thought Danielle would develop ulnar neuropathy in her elbow, a condition that afflicts the ulnar nerve, which runs from the neck to the hand and controls many of the muscles in the hand. The tests confirmed his suspicions, and he advised Danielle she would need surgery. He also said he needed to clean up the carpal tunnel scar tissue in her left wrist to alleviate some of the pain and numbness she had been experiencing. But the news didn't end there.

Danielle knew more was coming. She can't explain why, but she recalls that the room suddenly grew damp and cold. She realized the panic attack she'd suffered in Houston was associated with whatever bomb Dr. Black was about to drop on her world.

"Danielle, sit down," he said. Tears started to form in his eyes, and Danielle knew the news he was about to deliver would be terrible. "Danielle, you have a brain tumor."

"No. No, I don't. You're joking," Danielle said in disbelief.

Dr. Black showed her the scan and confirmed it was a brain tumor, probably a meningioma, which is usually benign. He told Danielle it was probably nothing to worry about, but she needed to see a specialist to confirm his diagnosis.

Danielle sat in Dr. Black's office and cried.

She recalls, "I had heard countless stories about other people suffering serious illnesses, but I never really thought it could happen to me. I felt as if I were hit by a truck and didn't know what to do."

Dr. Black sat with Danielle and consoled her as best he could. "We're going to get you set up with a great neurosurgeon," he said. "Call him to make an appointment as soon as possible. If they say they can't fit you in right away, call me. I'll handle it."

Dr. Black paused before continuing.

"Danielle, the radiologist who did your MRI called me himself to tell me about the tumor. He's concerned, too."

Danielle didn't respond to Dr. Black's instructions. Instead she asked whether the tumor was related to her RSD. Dr. Black said there was no correlation. The tumor was on the left side of her brain, which controls the right hand. Danielle's RSD issues affected the right side of the brain and left wrist. This tumor seemed to be completely random.

"Danielle, I'm serious," Dr. Black said sternly, as if talking to his own daughter. "You need to have this taken care of immediately."

Danielle nodded in agreement but still couldn't comprehend how she, a thirty-five-year-old woman, could be struggling with a brain tumor.

When she left Dr. Black's office, she made it as far as her car in the parking lot. She didn't know how she was going to drive home after hearing the devastating news. She called her parents to tell them, and her mother dropped the phone and began screaming when Danielle mentioned "brain tumor." Her dad started crying hysterically. Her mother didn't know what to do or how to help. She kept repeating, "You're kidding. You're kidding. You're kidding?" Danielle assured her mother she was not.

When Danielle hung up with her parents, she still didn't think she could drive home, so she called her boyfriend. When she told him she had a brain tumor, he thought she was joking. He refused to believe her and urged her to come home. When Danielle arrived, she showed her boyfriend the scan Dr. Black had given her. He could no longer deny the mass inside Danielle's brain. Neither of them knew what to do or how to act. Danielle spent the entire night in tears, not knowing what would happen next.

Following Dr. Black's instructions, Danielle called the neurosurgeon's office on multiple occasions to make an appointment, but no openings were available. She enlisted Dr. Black's assistance, and after he called the neurosurgeon himself, Danielle was given a slot for that same week.

Danielle drove herself to the office of Dr. Mark Weber after work that Friday. Not wanting to be alone when she learned her fate, she asked her boyfriend to meet her at the doctor's office. As Danielle sat in the examination room waiting to be seen by Dr. Weber, a nurse prepared her for the appointment. She told Danielle not to worry; the tumor did not appear to be in a difficult spot. Danielle felt a sense of relief. The nurse made it seem as if Danielle's case wasn't that serious and she wouldn't need surgery after all.

When Dr. Weber met Danielle, he painted a very different picture. He confirmed she had a meningioma, which was extraordinarily rare for people of Danielle's age. Tumors such as these usually take thirty to forty years to develop, so they typically appear in the elderly. Danielle hadn't experienced any of the usual symptoms, such as vision loss or balance problems. She would suffer from headaches occasionally, but those headaches usually accompanied bronchitis or a cold. Dr. Weber was baffled by how a tumor like this could form in someone so young so quickly and not give any warning signs. The tumor had formed sometime after 2010, when Danielle had her last brain MRI, which concerned Dr. Weber. Danielle's tumor was rather large, meaning it grew more rapidly than normal.

Danielle needed surgery, and she needed it quickly. Dr. Weber wanted to be as transparent with Danielle as possible, so he told her there was a chance she would not survive the surgery. Danielle appreciated Dr. Weber's candor, but the realization that she might never live a full life hit her hard. As she tried to process all the information she was given, she began to cry. Why her? Why now? She'd spent the last ten years dealing with various medical issues. Wasn't it time for her body to heal?

Dr. Weber stayed with Danielle for two hours, well after the office should have closed for the evening. He had a daughter of his own and could not imagine her going through something of this magnitude. He told Danielle, "I don't see people your age too often. I'm here for you." With those words, Danielle put all her trust in Dr. Weber. She made a mental note to cancel the appointments she'd previously scheduled with other neurosurgeons for second, third, and fourth opinions.

Dr. Weber scheduled Danielle's surgery for February 3, 2016.

In the two months leading to the surgery, Danielle tried to focus on living her life as best as she could. In December, she and her boyfriend drove to Miami for an art exhibit. While there, Danielle promised herself she would step out of her comfort zone and do things she normally wouldn't. She swam in the frigid ocean water, went to the Wynwood art district, soaked up the nightlife, and stayed up all night long. Danielle worried this might be her last chance at truly experiencing life, and she did not want to have any regrets.

"These weren't things I would typically do, but I felt my time was running out, and I needed to be sure I'd lived," she says.

As the calendar flipped to January, the days grew harder for Danielle. Her surgery date approached and her future seemed more finite than it once had. It seemed everyone in her life wanted to know more about Danielle's situation when Danielle just wanted to forget about it. On a whim,

Danielle decided she was going to name her tumor so she wouldn't have to always say the word *tumor* or *cancer*. From that day forward, she referred to her tumor as "Loretta."

"Giving my tumor an identity allowed me to cope. It made it easier to call it by a name since the name did not associate it with an illness," Danielle explains. "This made a tense time a little lighter. I even had a countdown to 'Loretta's eviction,' which made me smile and laugh a bit. My boyfriend and I would look at the calendar and say, 'Only three days until Loretta gets evicted!' I found a way to inject a little humor into my life during an otherwise bleak time, and that made all the difference."

The morning of Wednesday, February 3, finally came, and Danielle had to face her surgery. She was panicked and did not sleep well the night before. Knowing her fate would soon lie in the hands of her surgeon, Danielle broke down. She vomited from nervousness countless times that morning.

She arrived at the hospital at eight in the morning, but her surgery wasn't scheduled until one o'clock. This surgery required quite a bit of preparation, unlike her hand surgeries or tonsillectomy. In order to successfully remove Loretta, doctors had to map the exact location of the tumor prior to surgery. This was done using an MRI machine. The scan revealed that the tumor had grown since Danielle's diagnosis. If she had waited any longer to have the surgery, the tumor could have left her paralyzed, because as it grew, it had begun to press on the nerves that controlled mobility.

Danielle's surgery was supposed to last between five and six hours, but her doctor ran into some complications and it took him nine hours to remove the tumor. First Dr. Weber shaved a strip of Danielle's head from ear to ear. He decided not to shave her whole head because he knew how much she hated the word *cancer*, and he didn't want her to feel like a cancer patient when she awakened. Loretta had grown so large that the surgeon needed to break up some of the nerve endings in order to remove it. The tumor was much worse than anyone had imagined. Originally, Dr. Weber classified the tumor as Grade I, which meant it was benign. After it was removed, he changed his diagnosis to a grade three invasive meningioma, the worst kind. A Grade III meningioma grew abnormally fast and had the potential to spread throughout the brain and to other areas of the body. Danielle was truly fortunate to be alive.

Danielle's surgery finished at around ten o'clock at night. When she awoke, she had no recollection of who or where she was. Temporary memory loss often happens after the removal of brain tumors, though each patient has a different reaction. Danielle was transferred to the intensive care unit, where nurses kept her on a steady flow of morphine, so she was in a constant drug-induced state. She rarely opened her eyes or spoke. It was a waiting game to see how Danielle would react to the invasive surgery.

The following day, Danielle's boyfriend brought lunch from home. The night before surgery, Danielle had requested stuffed green peppers for dinner. It had been one of her favorite meals. Her boyfriend brought two leftover peppers wrapped in tinfoil and set them on the table in the ICU for when Danielle's mom was ready to eat. Upon smelling the pungent scent of peppers, Danielle screamed, "What is that f—ing smell? Get it out of here!" Her mother started chuckling and explained to the nurses how out of character it was for her daughter to curse. While Danielle's sudden aversion to stuffed green peppers amused her mother, it was another sign of how the tumor removal affected Danielle. Not only was it altering her personality, as evidenced by her uncharacteristic outbursts, it also affected her sense of smell and taste, a common occurrence with this type of surgery.

Danielle spent one night being monitored in the ICU. On Thursday, February 4, she was moved to a hospital room to finish her recovery. In order to move her from the ICU, nurses had to detach the central port and unhook all the monitors that tracked Danielle's progress. Unbeknownst to the staff at the time, Danielle suffered multiple seizures during the time she was off the monitors. These seizures caused her to lose her speech, though no one realized it initially because Danielle didn't say much while she was recovering. It wasn't until Sunday, the day she was to be discharged, that everyone noticed Danielle couldn't form sentences and didn't recognize her mother or boyfriend. The placement of her tumor, on the left side of her brain, had affected her communication and language skills. Her nurses began asking her various questions hoping to jog her memory and activate her speech. Danielle stared blankly at them. Her mom leaned down and whispered in Danielle's ear, urging her to answer the questions a certain way so they could all go home.

Even though Danielle was having post-op difficulties, her nurses recognized that she needed to leave the hospital for the comfort of her own home. The healing process might be expedited in a familiar setting. As a result, they discharged her that day. On the way home, Danielle's mother asked her if she was happy to be going home. Danielle answered by asking, "Who are you?" Her mother began to tear up, finally realizing that her daughter truly had no recollection of her.

"Nobody knows or can tell—not even doctors—how a brain surgery patient will be during recovery," Danielle says. "Each case is different. Everything was a fog in the hospital, so I really didn't know what was going on. All I knew was that once I left, it was going to be hard for everybody."

Indeed, recovery was slow for Danielle. She spent a month trying to regain her memory and speech. The only thing she recognized was her dog, Roman, but he wasn't allowed near her. Her memory loss frustrated her to no end. Danielle recalls, "When I realized I couldn't form words, I threw objects out of anger. I may not have remembered my life prior to this, but I knew this was not it."

Danielle's mother stayed in Orlando for a little more than two weeks to help care for her daughter, but when Danielle's sister delivered a baby in Houston, her mom flew back to Texas. At this point, Danielle could still not function on her own and relied on someone to help her walk and bathe and to drive her to her medical appointments. That heavy responsibility fell on Danielle's boyfriend. He washed Danielle's hair and braided it, tried to understand her garbled language, and became her sole source of support. Eventually, he needed to return to work, but since he worked the early shift, he was usually able to be home by 10:30 in the morning to resume his duty as caretaker.

Despite nearly two months of recovery time and daily physical therapy, Danielle was not improving. She still had difficulty walking and could not do so unassisted. She suffered from head pain, massive migraines, and anxiety. Danielle experienced frequent seizures and still had difficulty speaking. She was on a heavy regimen of medication to try to control each of these side effects, but her body did not cooperate.

Throughout the months of convalescence, Danielle felt she had only her boyfriend to rely on. She felt abandoned by her family in Houston and couldn't shake the sense that they had chosen her sister and her new baby over Danielle. Danielle didn't know how to cope with her loneliness, so she started looking for positives in her situation.

Danielle recounts, "I realized that I had learned a lot about myself through having a brain tumor. I never realized that I had been going through the motions of life without appreciating each day. Because of Loretta, I knew what life was about. I understood I may not have been healthy at that moment, but I still had a lot to offer. I learned how to live in the moment because I wasn't guaranteed tomorrow."

She decided to write a letter to Loretta, which took her five hours to compose, since she had just relearned how to write. In this four-page note, she wrote, "Dear Loretta, you are the best friend I ever had. You are the best roommate I ever had. What was the worst thing that ever happened to me, ended up being the best thing that ever happened. Thank you, Loretta."

Writing the letter allowed Danielle to release the anger she had been harboring toward her family. She understood that she could not change them, and she had to accept that. Expressing her thoughts on paper acted as a form a therapy. After not being able to express herself for months, and then not having anyone to talk to about how the changes affected her emotionally, this letter was Danielle's method of coping.

"Before writing the letter," Danielle says, "I had been angry all the time, not understanding what was happening to my body or what to do about it. I fought an internal battle and was losing. By writing everything down, I reassured myself that everything would be okay in my life, that I would be okay."

Once she scribbled all of her thoughts onto paper in her letter to Loretta, the ominous cloud that hung over Danielle drifted away, and she was able to start healing both physically and emotionally.

As part of her therapy, Danielle began taking classes at a school for people who needed to relearn life skills. Her instructors taught her how to do simple tasks in life, such as chopping vegetables, tying shoelaces, and fastening buttons. For quite a few months, Danielle could wear only leggings because she couldn't manage the buttons on a pair of jeans, a function most people don't even realize they perform naturally. This school played a huge part in developing Danielle's confidence.

"I was so connected to my teachers and therapists at my special school because they were with me the whole time I was relearning the basics; they understood what I was going through, whereas most other people in my life did not," Danielle says. "I basically had to start over and fast-track everything I had been learning my entire life, like how to get dressed, tie my shoes, and write my name. These teachers and therapists taught me something very important about myself, something I needed to learn at this stage in my life. They helped me realize that I had a name attached to my voice. I was a strong woman; I just needed to channel my energy into positive thinking, like learning how to write all over again and express myself."

Danielle also had to relearn how to walk, and she was determined to do so. At first, she used a walker and dragged her right leg limply behind her. With the help of daily physical therapy, Danielle regained her mobility, albeit slowly. Every step was a challenge, but Danielle yearned to regain her independence. During the summer of 2016, Danielle set a monumental goal to complete a 5K race at Walt Disney World. This was something she had always intended to do but had never accomplished. She thought this race would give her something to strive for when she needed it most. With the help of her physical therapist, Danielle improved step by step.

On November 4, 2016, Danielle, using a walker, lined up at the start of the Jingle Jungle 5K, alongside her physical therapist and boyfriend. Together, the three walked side by side for 3.1 miles through Disney's Animal Kingdom. Danielle pushed through the physical pain she suffered and the mental anguish she endured, with inner voices telling her she would never finish. Danielle did not falter. She thought about how just nine months earlier, doctors did not think she would ever walk again, how *she* never thought she would walk again. Each step made her stronger and bolstered her confidence. Danielle's life had changed drastically since the previous November. She shouldn't have been alive, but she was. Danielle pushed her walker across the finish line and felt an enormous sense of accomplishment.

"During my 5K, I realized how crazy an idea it was!" Danielle says. "I couldn't feel my legs. I was dizzy and afraid. But I also knew I was stronger than that fear, and I couldn't let it take over. If I let fear win and didn't finish the race, I worried about the person I would become. I didn't want to quit the race, and I certainly didn't want to quit my recovery.

I completed my 5K against all odds and have never been more proud of myself."

Danielle's mother waited for her beyond the finish line, carrying a sign of support from the entire family. Danielle felt that for the first time, her mom understood how hard Danielle's life had been over the last nine months.

Danielle remembers: "As I saw the blurred finish line ahead of me, there were very few cheerleaders remaining; the race was over, and only a few of us 'champions' were left to cross. I saw this little lady holding a neon poster board screaming and crying, and I knew at that very moment that my mom got it and was proud of me!"

Finishing the 5K gave Danielle a renewed sense of confidence. She still struggled with her speech daily and visited countless doctors weekly, but Danielle began to feel whole again after knowing that she could accomplish the goals she set. Her life was filled with optimism.

In December 2016, Danielle began to notice her boyfriend growing more and more distant. He would spend a lot of time away from home, and when he was home, he was always texting. Danielle grew suspicious that he was leading a double life. In February 2017, he came home from an annual trip to Costa Rica with his friends and told Danielle she had thirty days to move out. He had fallen in love with someone else, someone he had met at an art show the previous November. Danielle was devastated; how was she going to function now that the primary source of her physical and spiritual support was abandoning her? Panic soon set in; here she was, facing another huge obstacle. This obstacle came out of nowhere and had to be overcome quickly.

All Danielle's doctors were in Orlando and she was still being closely monitored by them, so moving to Houston to be with her family was not an option. She also knew she could not live alone, because even though she was more independent now, there were still a few things she needed help doing, such as getting around town. She could not drive, which meant she needed someone to transport her to her various appointments. She had relied on her boyfriend for so much, and maybe that was the problem. He had been her sole support for so long, perhaps he could not handle it any longer.

Not knowing where to turn, Danielle reached out to her friends on Facebook, hoping someone would have a room she could rent temporarily. Within minutes, a friend offered up his house. Danielle gladly accepted, and after putting her belongings in storage, she started her new, single life. She had lost her memory of all previous relationships so this breakup felt like the first one. It crushed her and sent her spiraling to a dark place. She sometimes wondered how the entire ordeal happened to her—the brain tumor, the difficult recovery, the breakup.

"I was very angry, upset, and confused and thought about ending my life multiple times even before I officially moved out of my apartment," Danielle says. "However, I was taking care of Roman solely at the time, and I looked into his eyes and knew I couldn't do it."

Danielle shifted her mind-set. She separated her medical life from her personal life. She vowed never to ask her new housemates to drive her to any appointments. She decided she could not rely on anyone as much as she once had relied on her now ex-boyfriend. She never wanted to feel as though she abused someone's kindness or that she had inconvenienced anyone. As Danielle took control, her spirits rose.

"I knew that after everything I had been through, the breakup couldn't break me," she says. "I survived brain surgery! What kind of quitter would I be if I did that? What about my voice? In that moment, I made a promise to Roman and myself that I would fight hard to become a better person and be strong for myself, because I learned then that nobody else would or could be for me.

"I had a necklace engraved that I wear every day with my tumor date in Roman numerals to remind myself of the promise Roman and I had made."

Today, Danielle is still recovering. She sees twelve specialists on a regular basis including her neurologist, pain specialist, psychologist, and speech therapist. She takes Uber rides to each appointment to solidify her independence. Though her tumor-removal surgery occurred in February 2016, Danielle still has issues with her speech and has to concentrate extremely hard in order to speak normally. She walks with the assistance of a cane or walker. Because the tumor was in the left side of her brain, the mobility in her right arm has not fully returned, and she continues to suffer from memory loss. While she still has seizures, they are rarer and milder through medication.

Danielle likes to joke that her life has been a constant headache since the time of her surgery in February 2016, and in reality, her migraines have grown more painful and last longer than ever before, sometimes for ten consecutive days. Her doctors worry that these increasing headaches could be related to more serious conditions, and they are sending Danielle for a two-week migraine study.

Danielle knows a new tumor could grow at any time, but she chooses to live her life without worrying about the future. Her focus is living in the moment. She has come to realize that there are only twenty-four hours in a day. If she has a bad day, she brushes it off, because the next day will be better. Her life is different post-brain surgery. She might not be able to jump in the frigid ocean waters anymore, but she still tries to live life to the fullest, even if that means just appreciating each moment.

Danielle McCarthy is fighting her fight every single day and succeeding. She believes she survived her ordeal for a reason: She wants to be a voice for those who do not have one. She dreams of writing a children's book about brain tumors and starting a brain tumor foundation named after Loretta. She wants people to learn from her experiences just as she will learn from them.

Danielle says, "People are going to have a bad day no matter who they are. My situation isn't any better or any worse than anyone else's. We all have different things going on. As people, we just need to learn how to get through the day as best we can. We need to love ourselves and be proud of who we are. We have to know that we are all strong."

Danielle will never understand why she developed a serious meningioma that almost took her life, but she's grateful for the unexpected trip to her hand doctor that saved her life. She survived when many do not, and she refuses to view her life through negative eyes.

"My future is a big sea of uncertainty, but I know that I am a survivor," says Danielle. "I wasn't proud of the me before the tumor. Even though I've gone through a lot, I'm a much better version of myself now."

Danielle's gratitude and positivity remind us that it's possible to find our footing after the worst trials of our lives, and though we don't know what the future holds for us, we have to continue to embrace each new day.

"Life is so precious," Danielle says. "Don't take things for granted. As long as you are the best person you can be and follow your heart, your life can be anything you want it to be, even after a traumatic event."

....

If you'd like to support an organization close to Danielle's heart, please visit the Florida Hospital Neuroscience Institute at floridahospital.com/foundation.

Margaret and Becky

"Heal women, heal generations."

Those are the words Becky Flood and her daughter, Margaret Smith, live by daily. The women approach each day with a mission: to help women and children whose lives have been torn apart by drug and alcohol addiction. It is a mission they undertook for deeply personal reasons. Becky has lived in recovery for forty-one years, and Margaret has witnessed the positive effects her mother's recovery has had on their family.

Alcoholism and addiction have coexisted in this family for generations. The link to addiction extends as far back as Becky's great-grandfather, who was known as the town drunk. Becky's grandparents on both sides felt the devastating effects of addiction but were highly functional, so the outside world never knew it. One grandfather was a functioning alcoholic who also suffered from sex addiction. His ex-wife, Becky's paternal grandmother, suffered from clinical depression. Becky's maternal grandmother, one of thirteen children, became addicted to prescription medications.

Many families in America have been affected by alcoholism, addiction, or mental health issues, and sadly they're afraid to seek help or ask for assistance. Becky is grateful to have been the first person in her family to speak up and out about addiction, and she feels blessed to have had a life of recovery. She says, "So many generations before us suffered in silence from addictive disorders and mental health issues. Today, that is no longer necessary. However, there is still stigma; luckily, it is not to the extent of what it used to be. The more of us that stand up and speak openly about recovery offer hope and pathways for others."

Neither of Becky's parents was an addict. In fact, they were the "hero" children, the ones who grew up to become successful adults with powerhouse careers and high salaries. They managed to avoid the vices that plagued their parents. Despite that, because the connection to drug and alcohol dependency was deeply rooted in her family tree, it's no surprise that Becky inherited the chronic brain disease known as addiction.

In the 1960s, when Becky was young, society didn't grasp the concepts of addiction or alcoholism the way it does now. It was common for women to rub whiskey on the gums of a teething baby or add a little bit to a bottle to help the baby sleep. So, when Becky went around finishing everyone's alcoholic beverages at a cocktail party at only two years old, no one thought much of it when they found her passed out behind the sofa. It seemed to be more laughable than concerning. There was no clear indication at the time that Becky would fall into the same addiction trap as the relatives before her; however, Becky was just nine years old when she intentionally got drunk for the first time. One Thanksgiving, the adults were drinking Scotch sours in celebration of the holiday. Becky's father had given the children a small amount of the alcoholic beverage as well, and Becky really liked the taste. Not understanding why the adults had larger glasses of the drink, she disappeared into the kitchen to fill her glass to the brim. When she finished the glass, she was so drunk she became the life of the party and the adults found it comical.

During her teenage years, Becky started drinking regularly, smoking pot, and using prescription pills. She was depressed, partly because she had dyslexia, which made school difficult, and also because she had naturally lower levels of endorphins and dopamine, making her less motivated to get through the day. To cope with her depression, Becky self-medicated. She found that the alcohol, marijuana, and pills helped her feel better, so she used more and more. It didn't help that Becky hung out with the wrong crowd, the ones who partied and fed her rebellious tendencies. She started acting out at school and twice wound up in the emergency room for intentional overdoses.

Luckily, her family paid attention to her behavior and recognized the changes in her personality. Her seventeen-year-old sister noticed that Becky's drinking was out of control and staged an intervention at their church youth group when Becky was only fifteen. This prompted Becky to attend Alcoholics Anonymous (AA) for the first time.

Meanwhile, Becky's parents observed her acts of self-destruction worsening and intervened. They sent Becky to a residential treatment facility in Bel Air, Maryland, where she remained for forty-five days. At the time, there were no adolescent treatment centers, so Becky attended this facility with only two other teenagers, aged thirteen and nineteen; the rest of the patients were adults. Today, Becky is the sole success story of those three teenagers. The other two passed away, one from an overdose and the other from cirrhosis of the liver.

Treatment was eye-opening for Becky. Even at her young age, she recognized that she had an abundant life full of love and opportunities, a life she did not want to throw away. Through the counseling she received in rehab, she learned how to feel good about herself without relying on drugs and alcohol.

"It's challenging for any adolescent to accept and understand the magnitude of having a fatal and incurable disease, let alone one that requires rethinking your whole way of life," Becky says. "I'm grateful to have had access to the best treatment available at the time and for my family that was fully committed and actively involved in my recovery. I could not have done it without my parents and siblings."

After leaving rehab, Becky understood she needed to avoid her temptations. She could no longer spend time with her old friends, who encouraged her bad habits. They continued to party, drink, and take drugs; they would surely continue to enable her addictions if she went back with them. Becky realized that in order to succeed in her recovery, she needed to seek out a new group, and she found her support in other recovering teenagers.

Becky also continued to attend AA meetings, both alone and with her family. She came to realize that because her family was actively engaged in the recovery process, she had the ability to come away from her addiction as a success story.

Of course, Becky recognizes that recovery is an ongoing, endless process. For forty-one years, she has lived one day at a time. Focusing on the present allows her to live in the moment without agonizing over or regretting her past. Becky credits her ability to stay focused on recovery to her spiritual journey, something AA strongly encourages.

"Addiction, like any chronic brain disease, can be emotionally and spiritually depleting, and one has to make a conscious effort to live a spiritual life to heal, whether that is through yoga, meditation, church, or even listening to music. Finding what fills you up spiritually is the defining factor of long-term success in dealing with a chronic illness," Becky explains. "When you are spiritually well, you are a human being who takes care of herself both emotionally and physically."

The Twelve-Step program used in AA is a spiritual journey in itself. The program references "God" or a "Higher Power" throughout the steps to remind those in recovery that some circumstances are beyond their control. Participants first admit to their addictions and understand the need to seek help from a "Higher Power." When they fully open themselves to that help, the healing and recovery begin. By the time they reach the twelfth step, not only have the participants committed to practicing spirituality on a daily basis, but they also understand the importance of continuing to carry the messages they learned to others in need.

Recovery does not become any easier, even after forty-one years of sobriety. But it does start to feel different. Becky lost the overpowering cravings she once experienced early in recovery. She warns that recovery can be mundane because of its necessary repetition.

"You wake up and follow the same routine day in and day out," she says. "You pray, do something fulfilling, and remind yourself that you have to help another human being that day. But the longer you are sober, the more you truly understand the deeper meaning of the Twelve-Step program."

Step Twelve of AA is: *Having had a spiritual awakening as the result of these Steps, we tried to carry this message to alcoholics, and to practice these principles in all our affairs.* In other words, in order to keep the sobriety and happiness that one learned in AA, one has to be willing to give it away to others. Early in her sobriety, Becky lived the twelfth step by helping to set up chairs or make the coffee before AA meetings. She started small, just as everyone did, but these acts of selflessness showed Becky how the spiritual journey was about other people, not solely about herself. As the years went on, Becky learned that daily acts of kindness were essential for recovery. The more she did for others, the happier she became.

Becky's dedication to recovery led her down a path that allowed her to use her experiences with addiction and sobriety to give back on a larger scale. After she got sober at fifteen, Becky went back to high school and trained to become part of the first group of adolescent peer counselors in her school. During her first few years of recovery, she volunteered with the Delaware Alcoholism Council, which then led her to earn a scholarship to attend Johns Hopkins University. There she became a certified addictions counselor, and she has been working in the field in some capacity since she was eighteen.

Becky spent twenty-six years working at a New Jersey treatment facility known as Seabrook House, where she was vice president of treatment services. At Seabrook House, Becky started MatriArk, a safe haven for pregnant women who came in for addiction treatment. Prior to MatriArk's establishment, pregnant mothers would be treated for their addiction on a short-term basis only; when they gave birth, they would not be allowed to stay in the center because there was no care available for the child. Becky knew this was detrimental to the well-being of the mothers and their children. MatriArk became a residential program where mothers and children could live together as the mothers sought help. It kept the mothers from having to choose between seeking treatment or staying with their children. It was a place where both mother and child were patients, because it provided psychological treatment for both. The campus had a childcare facility where each child had a clinician. The family was monitored over an extended period of time, which allowed a case manager to observe the mother in her actual living environment. Becky also ensured the campus offered parenting and bonding classes to teach the mothers how to be parents, a skill they had lacked while under the influence of drugs or alcohol.

Additionally, Becky worked to reunite mothers in the MatriArk program with the children they had previously lost due to their addictions. The women in treatment worked tirelessly to complete a drug or alcohol detoxification process. Then, once they could mentally and emotionally commit to sobriety, they were given more access to their children who were in the state's custody. This access started with supervised and weekend visits, then graduated to extended visitations until at some point the children were living on the MatriArk campus full-time with their mothers.

Eventually, Becky moved to California where, for thirteen years, she was the chief executive officer of New Directions for Women. New Directions for Women is a private, nonprofit rehab facility for women of all ages. Much like MatriArk, New Directions for Women also accepts children in the facility. The New Directions for Women staff understands that the entire family enters recovery together, so helping the children is just as important as helping the mothers.

Recently, Becky accepted an offer to become the president and CEO of Ashley Addiction Treatment Services in Maryland, which she says is serendipitous. She found her own sobriety in a Maryland treatment center. While there, she attended many lectures given by Father Joseph C. Martin, S.S., one of the primary founders of Ashley Addiction Treatment. To Becky, returning to Maryland feels as if her life has come full circle.

Becky never intentionally chose this career path; however, her devotion to recovery and living a spiritual life taught her that she wanted to be a source of help for people who needed it. She trusted that God would point her in the direction she should go, so she followed the paths that were laid out before her. Through this journey, Becky never backed down from hard work, a virtue her parents instilled in her at a young age.

She credits her parents for her successful recovery. If they hadn't been active in the process, Becky feels she never would have made the commitment to finding wellness when she did. If they hadn't raised her to uphold such high expectations of herself, she never would have understood that she *could* recover.

Becky decided to mother her own children in the same manner. She set high standards for them, but more importantly, she led by example. Margaret Smith, Becky's daughter, said her mother created a positive foundation for the family by believing in God, encouraging her children to volunteer and help others, and making light of even the worst situations, all values she committed to in her recovery. As Margaret would eventually learn, the Twelve Steps of AA enriched her own life just as they enriched her mother's.

Becky never hid the fact that she was in recovery; it was important for her to be honest with her children. When Margaret was very young, she knew her mother worked at a treatment facility, but it wasn't until she was older that Margaret understood the importance of that.

Unfortunately, Margaret's biological father also suffered from alcoholism but refused treatment. Even though her parents divorced when she was still young, Margaret witnessed the curse of addiction firsthand. She and her siblings attended Al-Anon meetings (for those affected by someone else's drinking) in support of their father. Once she realized her father would never choose sobriety, she stopped attending the meetings and severed ties with him. Through both Becky's teachings and her own knowledge of the Twelve Steps, Margaret understood the ramifications of addiction. Just as Becky had the courage to walk away from her enablers years before, Margaret chose to protect her own life by walking away from someone on the brink of self-destruction.

The knowledge that both her parents suffered from alcoholism was never lost on Margaret. As she entered her teenage years, she became more aware of where her choices could lead her. Margaret often worried she might become an addict because alcoholism plagued her lineage, and this awareness prevented her from straying too far from the rules.

Having a mother in recovery did not negatively consume Margaret's life. She and her siblings had very happy childhoods because they were able to focus on the positives, something they learned from their mother. Becky was a single mother for at least ten years. During that time, she worked multiple jobs, some of which were menial, just to pay the bills. Though Becky felt guilty for having to spend so much time providing for her family, Margaret and her siblings did not realize those were difficult times. Instead, they remembered playing games in the office building where Becky worked as a cleaner, and sitting on a couch with a bowl of popcorn watching movies as Becky counseled someone in the office next door. Those might have been difficult times, but the memories were full of love. Margaret saw the way her mother overcame her obstacles, and she realized she needed to emulate Becky's strength when faced with her own challenges.

Margaret's childhood set the tone for her future. Not only was she exposed to addiction and recovery in her own family, but she also witnessed how her mother's journey affected other people battling addiction. When she was twelve, Margaret began to volunteer at the daycare center at MatriArk and soon realized she wanted to devote her life to helping others just as her mother had done.

"It's not that I ever consciously made the decision to emulate my mom's strength, but I just naturally grew into it," Margaret says. "It's how I was raised, and I never knew anything different. It wasn't even an option to not be a helpful citizen and community member. After all, you are who you hang around with. I grew up instilled with the thinking that wherever and whenever there was a need, if you are able and capable of pitching in, you are responsible to do so."

Though she always envisioned herself working at a treatment facility like Becky, Margaret made the decision in college to study education instead. Because she'd never experienced addiction herself, Margaret worried she wouldn't be effective as a counselor or treatment professional.

So, she recalled the fond memories she had of working with children at MatriArk's daycare center and decided a career in teaching was her calling. When she volunteered at MatriArk, she noticed how the children born to addicted mothers required the most love and support. Margaret was instinctively drawn to helping them cope with their problems while their mothers were seeking treatment. Reflecting on her time at the daycare center, Margaret set a goal for herself. By her tenth year as a teacher, she wanted to be working with the most challenging children, the ones no other teachers wanted in their classrooms. Two years into her career, Margaret reached that goal. She became a special-education teacher in a behavioral-support classroom. The students she teaches were not able to be successful in the general-education setting and ultimately had to be removed from those classrooms.

"Some of the principles of AA are faith, courage, willingness, perseverance, and service—all of which show up in my journey of helping children and families," Margaret says. "Although I haven't worked the steps the way my mother has, the principles and core values have always been present in my life. I've worked to instill them in the children that I have the privilege of working with. In that way, the gifts of the Twelve Steps are being paid forward through my life."

Not only did Margaret choose a difficult career path, but she also chose to become a foster parent. The practice of opening her home to those in need was not new to Margaret. She can remember many times when Becky offered the family home as a refuge to mothers in recovery and their children. When Margaret was thirteen, Becky's friend and her three daughters came to stay at the house. During that time, the mother relapsed and was sent to rehab. The daughters, however, stayed with Becky's family until the mother entered recovery. Thus, having people come and go from her home never seemed unusual to Margaret.

While in college, Margaret worked full-time at a local hospital. One day, she was training a new hire who happened to be a foster parent. This woman mentioned that the demand for foster parents was extremely high in their county. Margaret had two children of her own at the time and knew she wanted more in the future but didn't necessarily want to give birth to them. Because she had always felt drawn to helping children in need, fostering seemed to be a good fit, and Margaret kept the idea in the back of her mind for the future.

Three years later, her son had a tonsillectomy at that same hospital. When Margaret approached the nurses' station to get him some pain medicine, she noticed a baby's bassinet behind the counter and joked, "Hey, what's a baby doing here? Shouldn't he be over in the maternity ward?" The nurses explained that the mother had given birth and left the baby alone at the hospital with no intention of returning for him. The staff was waiting for social services to find the newborn a foster home. Margaret asked how often something like that happened and was told, "All the time." This particular baby had been at the hospital for three or four days at that point, and there were no open foster homes in which to place him. When a situation like this occurred, the hospital kept the babies in its care until a home was available.

This event sparked something in Margaret. She struggled with the idea of a mother not loving her child. She had received a great deal of love from her mother, and she had given a lot of love to her own son and daughter as well. The thought of a mother leaving her child without a safe place to call home struck Margaret's heart. She told her husband about the incident, and they agreed they needed to act. Soon after, they contacted their local social services department to become licensed foster parents. Over the last nine years,

Margaret and her husband have fostered thirty-three children, most of whom were placed into the system because of addicted parents. They have adopted four of their foster children, joining their two biological children.

Margaret looks at fostering through two lenses. It can be fantastic and rewarding, but at the same time, it can be very challenging because of a flawed system. Often, foster children are reunited with biological mothers who are not remotely close to being responsible authority figures. The system gives the biological parents chance after chance to reunite with their children; however, it does not provide the parents with therapy, appropriate treatment for their addictions or mental illnesses, or adequate parenting classes. Without this help, the parents fall back into their old ways and the children become victims again.

"Consistency is necessary for children to thrive," Margaret says. "Bouncing between biological parents, who may not be ready to be parents, and foster homes will always cause children to suffer emotionally. I hope that the entire system—lawmakers, governors, mayors, as well as the governmental services themselves—can change the policies and procedures that are in place to do what is best for the child, every time."

Margaret feels that fostering is a great challenge emotionally. There are times she thinks there is no way she can do it anymore, that she cannot put her heart through more agony. With fostering come so many unknowns: Will the child embrace the family? Will the entire family embrace the child? How long will the child stay? Margaret explains how this might be the most difficult part of fostering.

"During the adoption process, it is very possible for the biological mother to recover from addiction," she says. "You raise these kids for two years and want to adopt them. On one hand, you love them and consider them your own children; on the other hand, you realize how amazing it would be if their biological mother did get well."

Fostering is fraught with challenges. Children who are exposed to drug use have a higher risk of mental instability or behavioral problems. Often, children surrounded by addiction suffer from abuse or neglect, thus creating an unstable foundation at a tender age. Entering the foster care system and moving around from home to home can cause an already unsettled child to become aggressive.

Margaret makes a conscious effort to do check-ins with her entire family, including the foster children. She asks herself if everyone's needs are being met. *Is everyone getting the help they need? Can we provide this help? Or do we need to allow someone else to take over who can provide specialized care?* Asking these questions makes Margaret an outstanding foster parent. Some people treat the kids who come into their homes like visitors rather than part of the family. Margaret sees her role as an advocate for the children who require additional help. She and her husband try to do the best they can not only for these children but also for the children's mothers. Margaret offers advice and tries to point social services in the right direction so these women can seek assistance with their addictions.

Yes, fostering can be difficult, but Margaret hopes to be the light in these children's lives, the person who helps them realize that they don't have to fall into the cycle of addiction and that they have the ability to choose a life different from what they grew up with. Margaret hopes she has shown them this alternative life and that they will feel inspired to continue living well when they leave her care.

Margaret has some advice for people who want to begin fostering: "Do it! It's amazing. You have to be a very strong person to do it and do it well. Be open-minded and willing to self-reflect. Every child will have a different need because they have different personalities. Likewise, you should have different expectations of them. Fostering changes you. It makes you more thoughtful and grateful, more willing to help others and see your own blessings. You may be changing the lives of these kids, but they're also changing yours."

Becky Flood and Margaret Smith have seen the effects of alcoholism and addiction. They also have witnessed the benefits of recovery and commitment to a life of selflessness. They continue to serve their communities by offering safe havens for those affected by addiction. They offer messages of hope and promises for better lives. They will never stop their missions, because addiction follows a cycle through the generations. Both Becky and Margaret work to break this cycle in their own ways, one with mothers, the other with children.

Their message is clear: "When we provide mothers with the resources to heal from their addictions, they can give their children a chance at a meaningful and healthy life. Otherwise, the addiction tragedy continues, from generation to generation."

....

If you'd like to support an organization close to Becky's heart, please visit New Directions for Women at newdirectionsforwomen.org.

....

If you'd like to support an organization close to Margaret's heart, please visit CASA of Cecil County, Maryland, at cecilcasa.org.

Monique

Ever since she was fourteen years old, Monique Gilliam has started her morning with a simple mantra: "Today is going to be a great day."

Monique's positivity actually stems from family tragedy and has carried her through some of the most difficult times of her life, which have included the deaths of several loved ones, homelessness, and hopelessness.

So what events led young Monique to embrace the positives in her life? Her parents separated soon after she was born because her father abused alcohol and marijuana. Monique's mother didn't want her daughter raised in that environment. Though her mother never spoke ill of Monique's father, he was not a part of their lives after the separation.

In April 1993, when Monique was only thirteen years old, her father was shot and killed when he and her uncle intervened in a neighbor's domestic violence incident. Though Monique could count on one hand the number of interactions she had with her father, this sudden loss devastated her because she had been working on developing a relationship with him.

As if the passing of one parent wasn't enough for a teenage girl, Monique's mother attempted suicide for the first time in June 1993. That day, when Monique arrived home from school, she found her house buzzing with family members. Monique was told that her mother tried to hurt herself and was in the hospital, but no further details were given. She didn't ask questions, nor did anyone offer further explanation. Monique's mother survived the attempt, which prevented Monique from losing both parents within a two-month span.

Most people, especially those in their early teens, would have difficulty dealing with the death of one parent and the attempted suicide of another. But Monique did not let these incidents get the better of her. She never asked God why she had to deal with death during her formative years. Instead, she developed a strong, positive outlook, one that would propel her toward her best self. She reminded herself that she had the power to create a great day.

"My father's death and mother's first suicide attempt occurred when I was still thirteen years old. I didn't turn fourteen until July, and after the previous events, I was determined to have a great school year," Monique recalls. "So, when school started in late August, I started and ended my day with a talk with God. I didn't get on my knees with my hands folded and eyes closed; I simply talked to God. I would talk out loud about my day, fears, goals, essentially everything. And the funny thing is, I knew God was listening. The twist was that no matter what, I claimed each day to be a good day, and typically it was, no matter what I

was going through. I noticed the power I had by controlling my thoughts, and while I may not have been in control
of the world around me, I could control how I reacted in it."

Monique was raised in an urban neighborhood in
Cincinnati, Ohio, called Over-the-Rhine. It used to be an
area known for its deteriorating historic architecture, low-
income housing, and high crime rate. But Monique's mother
always reminded her, "It's not about where you live. It's about
how you live."

Though her mother struggled to provide Monique and
her two younger brothers with what she thought was the
ideal life, she gave them more than she realized. For starters,
she taught Monique the meaning of hard work. Monique's
mother was at one point a maid, but she had an entrepre-
neurial spirit and worked her way through a myriad of jobs,
even becoming a mortgage loan officer. Monique saw in her
mother a deep love and a fighting spirit that wanted to keep
improving her family's quality of life.

Monique's mother also raised her children in a diverse
atmosphere. Monique is African American, but her home
was a haven for people of all races and ages. Her mother's
various jobs introduced Monique to friends from all walks
of life. Her grandmother volunteered with a group of nuns,
mostly white, known as the Dominican Sisters of the Poor,
and Monique's family would attend their gatherings on a
regular basis. Monique was raised in a family that not only
valued love and acceptance but also embodied it.

Monique never considered her family to be poor. They didn't have a lot, but they were afforded more opportunities than most people she knew. Monique was never a product of her environment. She became involved with activities like Girl Scouts and writing clubs. She attended private school from first through twelfth grades, even earning a scholarship to a prestigious private high school. Upon graduating high school, she went straight to college. In Monique's eyes, she had all she needed growing up.

As she grew older, times became more trying. When Monique was sixteen, her mother attempted suicide for the second time. Her mother had locked herself in the bathroom and slit her wrists. Her mom's boyfriend at the time broke down the door and found her bleeding. In a state of shock, he ran away. Monique stayed with her mother, and even though her mother pleaded with Monique to let her die, Monique could not allow that to happen. She called for help and had her mother taken to a hospital, where she stayed for a week. During this time, it was Monique's responsibility to care for her two younger brothers. She got them to and from school, fed them, and made sure their needs were met. Though other family members came by from time to time to check on the three siblings, they were ultimately on their own.

For most of her young life, Monique hadn't realized that her mother suffered from mental illness. It wasn't until after she returned home from the hospital after the first suicide attempt that her mother opened up about her manic depression. Unfortunately, her mother was not the only person in the family dealing with psychological issues. Monique's brother Sherman was diagnosed with bipolar and manic-depressive disorders at just twelve years old. Around the time of his diagnosis, he tried to commit suicide for the first time by overdosing on his mother's pills. He was transported to a hospital and had his stomach pumped. It was disheartening for sixteen-year-old Monique to know her little brother was in such emotional turmoil that he wanted to end his life. She felt she should have seen the signs or done something more to protect him.

In reality, there was nothing more anyone could have done to save Sherman. Four years later, when he was sixteen, he succeeded in ending his life. Monique was a college sophomore at the time.

What many people regard as the best years of their lives became some of the darkest in Monique's. College should have been a time of personal growth and freedom. Instead, it was marked by some of the greatest losses of her life. During her freshman year, Monique's beloved great-grandmother passed away. Then she lost Sherman in May 1999. Just before Monique began her junior year, in the summer of 1999, her grandmother passed away from AIDS. And on December 31, 2000, Monique's mother finally succeeded in ending her life.

"The tragedies I had to deal with were dealt with in those specific moments. I didn't carry visible baggage, so to speak,"

Monique says. "I learned to accept what I couldn't change. I was most certainly saddened by the course of events, but I still had to live, and so that's what I chose to do. I embraced each day with a smile on my face. People were always impressed by what they perceived to be this superhuman strength. Everyone has a story; everyone is struggling with something. Everyone has something they must conquer. I was no different."

But the tragic events changed Monique. She searched for a way to fill the void each loss had left in her heart, and she turned to relationships to mend her brokenness. In early 2002, she had been in a nearly two-year relationship with a man and they were expecting their first child. Just over five months into her pregnancy, however, Monique's water broke; she was immediately admitted to a hospital. She developed a one-hundred-four-degree fever and was in excruciating pain. Her body acted as if the unborn child were an infection, and it was trying to push it out. As Monique lay in the hospital bed on pain medication, a nurse lifted the covers and noticed she was starting to deliver the baby. Monique was petrified; she knew she shouldn't go into labor for at least another three months. It was too soon. The baby would be too underdeveloped to survive.

Monique gave birth to her son three and a half months prematurely. He had no chance for survival, but Monique was allowed to hold him for a moment. She stared down at the tiny baby in her arms wishing she had more time with him. He was so young that his organs and external features were not fully developed. His ears were tiny and his lungs were barely functioning. She watched as he opened and closed his mouth like a fish trying to take in air.

As her eyes and heart took in all of her son, Monique's mind circled back to something her mother once told her: "I hope you never know what it is like to lose a child." After Monique's brother committed suicide, her mother had a difficult time dealing with his death. In Monique's mind, her mother was not the only person who had suffered the loss. His death affected many. She told her mom, "You lost a son, true. But I lost a brother; people lost a friend."

Monique could not comprehend how this single loss could destroy a person. Now, here she was cradling her firstborn child, a child who would die before he ever had the chance to live. And at that moment, Monique understood the weight of her mother's words. Losing a child was an incomprehensible pain, one she would have to carry the rest of her life. After the harrowing ordeal, Monique left the hospital with an irreparable crack in her heart.

A couple years after the loss of her first son, Monique gave birth to a healthy baby boy and her life as a mother began to take shape. By 2006, Monique had separated from her son's father. She was juggling being a single mother to a three-year-old boy and working in the medical records department of a Cincinnati hospital when both she and her son suffered from severe flu-like symptoms. She took her son to the emergency room of the hospital where she worked to be checked by a doctor. While there, Monique ran into her supervisor, who advised her not to come into work the next day. Monique obliged; however, she didn't officially call in to her office to report her absence because she had discussed the matter with her boss the previous day. As a result of her failure to call in, her absence was considered a "no call, no show," which, according to company policy, was grounds for termination. Monique lost her job.

Monique was not prepared to lose her steady stream of income. Without her job, she could no longer afford her car, necessities for herself and her son, or even rent. Suddenly, Monique found herself a single mother without a place to live. She and her son were homeless. Monique had taken pride in being independent and in being able to provide for her family. Not having the means to do so was heartbreaking. For a brief moment, she felt discouraged and embarrassed by her homelessness.

Once Monique came to terms with this new obstacle in her life, she did the only thing she knew how to do when times were rough: She stayed positive. She said to herself, *Okay, this is the situation. How can I make it better?* Monique instantly began looking for ways to turn her life around. Her uncle told her about a local shelter called Bethany House, whose services were exactly what Monique needed.

Bethany House is a shelter for women and their children. At the time, it was a single house, and each family had its own bedroom. Perhaps one of the best features of this shelter was the daily structure. Every morning, the expectation was that the children would go to daycare or school and the mother would go to work, go to look for a job, or go to school. There was a curfew in place; everyone had to be home by dinnertime unless someone had a job that conflicted. On weekends, residents weren't required to leave the premises, but the shelter expected that they make plans and be productive as opposed to just sitting around all day.

Bethany House also had a plan to set up its residents for success. Once the mother found a job, the shelter managed the bulk of her income and placed it into a savings account for the family. When the family was ready to move out of the shelter, Bethany House used that savings to provide a deposit and first month's rent for a new apartment.

Monique knew she would benefit from living at Bethany House and put her name on the waiting list. After a week, she and her son were accepted into the facility and moved in.

Monique entered this phase of life with a game plan. She was going to take full advantage of living in a place that had her best interests at heart. The support motivated her to improve her life. She immediately set out to look for a job and within two weeks was back to working full time. The following week, she found an apartment to rent. After only thirty days of living at Bethany House, Monique was able to put down a security deposit and three months' rent.

When starting her life at the shelter, Monique again put her mom's words into perspective: "It's not about where you live. It's about how you live." Monique made the best of living at Bethany House and used her resources so she could close that chapter of her life.

Since her time at Bethany House, Monique has worked several jobs, largely because she created her own opportunities. The job she landed in 2006 while living in the shelter was as an executive assistant for a one-man company. At the time, the owner of the company was not even looking to hire an assistant, but Monique wowed him with her skills and convinced him to hire her. After more than two and a half years, he could no longer afford to pay Monique, so he had no choice but to let her go.

Monique next convinced a local artist that she should be his manager, and he agreed; however, his business was funded by individual grant-holders, and once those people reallocated their funds to other artists, he could no longer pay Monique's salary. After nine months, Monique once again found herself without work.

Though Monique had enjoyed her previous two jobs, she realized she needed to work for a more reliable company, one that would consider her to be an indispensable employee. In May 2009, Monique interviewed for a financial aid position at the Art Institute of Cincinnati and impressed the interviewers with her dynamic, can-do attitude, determination to succeed, and her résumé. They hired her on the spot.

This job became a turning point for Monique. Still a single mother, her previous jobs had not paid well enough for Monique to save much. When she'd lost the last job, she had been forced to rely on relatives for a place to live. This new position allowed Monique to move back into her own apartment and slowly rebuild her savings. The job also taught her the value of networking in order to advance her career, something that would become useful in the future.

Monique's life improved over the next two years. She had a stable job that kept her busy and fulfilled. She spent ample time with her budding family, which now included a son and daughter. She met a man and had another child. But as fate would have it, this man turned out to be emotionally abusive, and by the summer of 2011, Monique was eager to end the nearly two-year relationship and move out. But Monique was pregnant, and due to her past financial problems, including a large delinquent energy bill, she was having trouble finding an apartment for her and her children to move into, thus making it difficult to end the relationship.

"I didn't see my relationship as being abusive, at first," Monique says. "When I think of an abusive situation, I think of one that involves endlessly yelling and screaming accompanied by frequent beatings. My situation wasn't like that, and it wasn't until my relationship ended that I saw how volatile it could've been. The abuse crept in slightly. It started with isolation; he frowned upon family coming to our home. He would put me down, discourage me from accomplishing goals. At one point, he even disrespected my mother, a woman he never met. The final straw for me was when he choked me. I don't even really know what possessed him to do it; I just knew I wouldn't make myself available for him to do it again. I refused to allow my children to grow up in an environment of abuse or violence of any magnitude."

Monique, being an upbeat and gregarious individual, had developed a friendship with her children's pediatrician, Shana. During one visit to the office, Monique had confided in Shana about her financial struggles, difficulty finding a new apartment, and the need to end an abusive relationship. Shana offered to help Monique hunt for a new place to live so she could cut ties with her partner. The two women drove all around Cincinnati and the surrounding areas looking for apartments Monique could afford on her own. They looked in various areas, including the worst neighborhoods where shootings often occurred. That was when Shana offered to have Monique and her children move in with her family, which included a husband and two children. Monique was hesitant at first. She did not want to burden Shana's family, knowing that having her family there would double the amount of people living under one roof. Though Shana had been Monique's pediatrician for years, their friendship was only just beginning, and Monique did not want to destroy it by imposing her life on to Shana's. Ultimately, Monique took Shana up on her offer and their families blended under one roof beginning August 2011.

Monique considers Shana to be an angel whom God placed into her life for a reason. Not only did Shana open her heart and home to someone she was just starting to know on a personal level, she also helped to ensure Monique stayed strong, positive, and hopeful, and she introduced Monique to an organization geared toward single mothers— MomsHope. The mission of MomsHope is "to provide hope to single, low-income moms through one-on-one faith-based mentoring in order to support their resource development, personal advancement, spiritual growth and family stability." In October 2011, Monique was given a mentor, and in December 2011, MomsHope paid half Monique's overdue electric bill, which allowed her to finally find her own apartment.

Much like when she lived at Bethany House, Monique had entrusted Shana and her husband with a portion of each paycheck so she was guaranteed to have savings for an apartment when the time came. In December 2011, Monique and her children moved out of Shana's house and into their own apartment, where they still reside. It was difficult for Monique to leave Shana. They had developed a strong bond over the months and Shana kept asking if they really wanted to leave. But Monique was eager to be on her own again and not feel like a burden to her friend's family.

Moving day was on a Saturday and Monique had to work. Shana told her not to worry. She enlisted the help of her friends and moved what little belongings Monique owned (she had gotten rid of a lot upon moving in with Shana) into the new apartment. When Monique walked into her new home after a long day at work, she was shocked to see what her friend had done. Not only had Shana moved Monique's belongings from point A to point B, but she also had gathered furniture donations from friends so Monique had a fully furnished apartment. Shana had organized the rooms, bought groceries, and even decorated a Christmas tree for the family. The only thing Monique had to do was unpack her clothes. Monique believed that was an act of the truest friendship on earth, a friendship she treasures to this day.

Even though she had moved into her own apartment and her life was normalizing, Monique continued her relationship with MomsHope and her mentor there. Knowing that she wanted to continue to advance in the workplace, Monique showed her mentor her résumé and a rave review written by her boss at the Art Institute. Though Monique was still employed, her mentor lined up an interview for Monique at her high-end real estate firm. Monique's efforts paid off, and in September 2013, she signed on as a property administrator for that firm, earning her highest salary since entering the workforce.

One negative aspect of the new job, however, was the homogenous, elite air in the office. Monique thrived on diversity and collaboration. It was how she was raised; it was the atmosphere in all of her previous jobs; it was the real world. Prior to her first day at the real estate firm, her mentor said, "I want to tell you, do not disclose who you are or what you've been through." She did not want Monique's coworkers to know that she had once lived in a shelter and struggled financially. Though Monique knew her mentor was only trying to help, that statement sent chills down her spine. Every experience of adversity she had faced had made Monique more resilient. She was not ashamed of her past, but her mentor made it seem as if she should be. Her journey made her who she was. Reflecting on her mentor's comment, Monique says, "It has made me the beautiful person that I am, and for someone to say that it is shameful, it hurt me."

Her mentor's words were a catalyst for everything that followed. Monique automatically put up a wall and did not walk into the new job as herself. She was forced to put up a façade from the very beginning. Monique immediately knew she did not fit in the corporate environment. The office lacked diversity. She was surrounded by white men talking loudly on their headsets as they swung their golf clubs. Monique was one of just three Black employees in the office. It seemed that everyone in the office kept her at a distance. When she went to work functions, her colleagues did not mingle with her. She was made to feel like she didn't belong in their corporate world. Monique found this behavior to be belittling and hurtful.

The destructive atmosphere slowly took its toll on her. Earning a high salary was great for her family and her savings, but Monique longed for something fulfilling. She felt underappreciated and needed a way to give back to the community. In November 2015, two years after she started working at the real estate firm, Monique began volunteering at Bethany House, the shelter that once saved her. She and some friends went to the shelter to cook a meal for the residents one night. Monique found that activity to be so rewarding that she went back again to see how else she could help. She wanted to find a way in which she could make a bigger, more lasting impact than just cooking a meal. She sat down with the women residents and found out what they needed. They told Monique they needed help finding employment. That sparked an idea in Monique. When she lived at Bethany House, there had been a case manager who helped women find an initial job and an apartment, but there was never anyone available to expand on that. These women needed help setting short- and long-term goals and then executing the plans to reach those goals. They needed assistance writing résumés and filling out financial aid forms. The shelter did not provide these services.

Monique might not have been in the exact place she wanted to be with her own job, but she felt she could help lift up other women as she herself was being lifted; volunteering brought fulfillment to her life. In June 2016, Monique developed a proposal and presented it to the director of Bethany House. She offered to come into Bethany House, which by then had three living establishments, and help women with their résumés, career planning, financial planning, educational planning, and long-term goals. Her goal was to come to the shelter to help other women get a leg up on their situations.

The director loved Monique's ideas and allowed Monique to provide her expertise and assistance. Monique quickly began trying to execute her plan. But her volunteer work started to add more stress to her life. Monique was constantly rushing around. She would work her full-time job, pick up her children from school, and then volunteer at the shelter from six to nine at night. Sometimes she would find herself getting aggravated while at the shelter because some of the residents did not want to work to improve their situations. Monique was trying to fulfill her life's purpose by helping these women, but she felt stuck when they did not want to change their lives. Monique also felt guilty that she was spending too much time away from her children when she volunteered. She hoped they one day would be able to be a part of this mission with her, but at the moment, she was on her own.

In September 2016, Monique's world came to a screeching halt. She noticed one day at work that her brain seemed cloudy and foggy. Her hands would not stop shaking. She could not think logically, and she was overcome with hopelessness. Though she admitted she had previously questioned the reason for her existence on this earth, she never once thought about suicide until that day. Monique knew her emotional state at that moment was fragile.

"I felt like I had a calling to do more and couldn't. I started to question my life and its purpose," Monique recalls. "I was going through a mental battle. One side of my brain said, 'Life would be easier if you weren't in it,' while the other side of my brain said, 'Don't give up. God's not done with you yet.' After losing my mother and brother to suicide, I know how crippling that experience can be. I would never want to put my family and friends through that kind of turmoil. Knowing that I was out of my mind, so to speak, I did the right thing and decided to ask for help."

Because she worked for the hospital division of a real estate firm, her office was actually located inside a Cincinnati hospital. She walked down to the mental health floor, explained to some nurses exactly how she felt, and told them she needed help. Though Monique had just hoped to speak with someone, the staff immediately checked her into the hospital and put her under suicide watch. They would not let Monique leave, which left her even more discouraged and frightened. She feared losing her job again.

That day, Monique had felt mentally unwell and hopeless with no one to turn to, and she knew she needed help. She was being proactive by seeking out someone with whom she could speak. She hadn't expected to be admitted. She was frustrated that she did what she thought was right by reaching out for help but ended up being treated like a dangerous person who needed to be held in a straitjacket.

"My idea of help would have been for me to have an

evaluation, arrange to regularly meet with someone like a counselor, and receive prescribed medication if the doctors deemed it necessary," Monique says. "Instead, I was treated like I had taken an overdose of medication. I had not physically harmed myself in any way, and I was put on watch with a guard outside my door like I was a madwoman. The entire experience was a real nightmare."

Monique remained in the hospital for a week. The first few days, she was resistant and upset with herself. She kept scolding herself: *I have a job to do; I let my kids down.* Then she had an epiphany. This was God's way of allowing her to have some quiet time. The mental health floor had group therapy sessions and Monique actively participated. She utilized the situation to her advantage. Instead of focusing on how she got there, she was mindful of why she was there and how she could benefit from being there. She realized she had wound up in the hospital for a reason and she needed to get well for her children.

After a week, Monique urged the hospital to release her since she had to return to her children and her job. The day she left, she felt as if she had been incarcerated for years. She stepped outside and the fresh air hit her face. Monique felt relieved and happy. She wanted to live. She wanted to get back to life.

Monique returned to her daily routine, and although she had a new zest for life, her work environment continued to swallow her whole. In May 2017, the real estate firm laid off Monique, but for once, she felt more relief than fear. She quickly realized that her termination was a blessing. She felt that God saw she was unhappy and intervened on her behalf.

Since she lost her job, other doors opened for Monique. United Way approached Monique to speak at one of its events about her experiences while living at Bethany House. Monique, with ample time to give back to her community, willingly accepted. She spoke to an audience of six hundred. Monique reveled in the experience and plans to continue with her public speaking. She is in her element when she shares her story.

MomsHope also approached Monique with an opportunity to share her experiences with their community. She came to one of their meetings and offered her insight. The following morning, the director of MomsHope contacted Monique and told her how much they benefited from having her in the meeting. Once again, Monique saw the fruits of her labor and realized she had a new purpose in her life: to use her personal experience with homelessness to bring about hope and change for others in similar situations.

Monique understands that simply telling her story isn't enough to enact change; she knows she has to be hands-on in order to make the greatest impact in her community. She is actively working to turn the project inspired by her work at Bethany House into something much larger. She plans to turn it into a nonprofit organization that will work with several shelters and halfway houses. No more than two weeks after losing her last job, Monique received an invitation from Mortar, a nonprofit organization that caters to low-income entrepreneurs who have a desire to start their own businesses, to join their eleven-week class. She was given a mentor along with the tools needed to start her business. Monique is looking forward to making headway on this project, which she hopes one day will be a family affair shared with her four children.

Sharing her story of overcoming homelessness has allowed Monique to bring awareness and hope to those in similar situations. In November 2017, she was nominated for the Jimmy Render award. Given through the Greater Cincinnati Coalition for the Homeless, this award acknowledges someone for his or her role in fighting to make a difference for those affected by homelessness. Additionally, Monique began a new career in January 2018 as the director of community strategy for the Cincinnati City Council. This position has allowed her to be directly involved in generating more attention for the needs of displaced families and those battling mental illness.

Monique always knew that what you put out into the universe is what you get back, which was why she always chose to stay positive even in her darkest hours. She realizes that each of her trials has added to her personal growth. Monique believes that no matter what life throws at her, she can handle it. She has conquered so much already and continues to look at the bright side of each day. Her life is too important to her to focus on the negative. Monique wants everyone to remember that we will all have both good and bad days throughout our lives. The good are much more prevalent; therefore, those are the ones we need to keep in focus.

Monique Gilliam is a force in her community. She lends her voice to the voiceless, and that voice is not only heard but also fiercely admired. Her life might have been turbulent at times, but she derives her strength from those challenging moments.

"It goes without being said that I am who I am because of the woman who raised me," Monique says. "My mother taught me at a very young age the importance of faith, humility, service for others, and most importantly, love. After the loss of my mother, a part of me died. My mother always saw the greatness in me, and I've learned that sometimes it takes others to see the greatness in you in order for you to see the greatness in yourself. I've spent the last seventeen years finding myself. It's been one heck of a journey. Life is good, and it's only going to get greater. I have learned that one's mindset is everything, so no matter what, keep it light and keep it positive."

....

If you'd like to support an organization close to Monique's heart, please visit MomsHope at moms-hope.org.

Christina

"No fear is worth losing your dreams over," Christina Anston explains. And Christina knows fear.

By the time she was eleven years old, she had moved eight times. As Christina grew older, her family would lose its home due to arson and suffer from financial ruin. Christina would endure homelessness, care for seriously ill loved ones, and ultimately face her own mortality after a frightening diagnosis.

Christina Anston knows fear. She simply refuses to give into it.

Having been uprooted so many times as a child, Christina experienced many significant losses in her young life. She was constantly having to adjust to change: new houses, new bedrooms, new schools, new friends, new countries and cities, new time zones, different accents, and different customs. Without coping skills or the verbal skills to express her feelings, Christina struggled with extreme anxiety from an early age—which is ironic, because she comes from a family of mental health professionals. Her father was a notable psychiatrist; her mother was a psychiatric nurse.

Christina first experienced anxiety around age six. She was living in England and in first form at school—otherwise known as kindergarten in Christina's native Canada—when she became so anxious that she felt dizzy and developed blurred vision. She screamed in terror as she feared that she was going blind.

After moving back to Canada a few years later, Christina developed heart palpitations. Her heart beat so fast from anxiety, she thought she was having a heart attack. She often thought she was dying and demanded to be seen by a doctor. "Call the ambulance!" twelve-year-old Christina yelled to her mother. "I'm having a heart attack!"

Knowing Christina's fear would continue to escalate if ignored, her mother brought her to a hospital to be examined by a cardiologist. Convinced she would need to be admitted to the hospital for observation or a heart transplant, Christina packed an overnight bag. Once the cardiologist examined her and assured her she was not having a heart attack, Christina leapt off the exam table as if she had been miraculously cured.

"I was such an anxious child, I needed reassurance," Christina recalls. "My mother worried excessively about her children's health, too, and although she had become accustomed to my physical symptoms related to anxiety, she always took me seriously, just in case that time it was not just in my head. My father, on the other hand, would send me for one test appropriate for whatever I complained about. When he got the all clear, that was all he needed to tell me that similar symptoms were all in my head. He was only wrong once. My car sickness was not all in my head but on the back seat of his Camaro!"

Those affected by anxiety do not see their fears as being irrational; it's not a switch that can just be flipped to the off position. The fear of having a heart attack or of finding out the lump on her forehead was cancerous were very real threats to Christina, and she couldn't rid herself of those thoughts.

Sometimes, when Christina was in school, her anxiety would not allow her to concentrate in the classroom. Nervous energy would accumulate in her body, derailing her focus. Her throat would become tight and dry, and Christina would grow more distracted. Then, she would worry about upcoming exams, fearing she probably missed something important in class.

Though she participated in athletics, such as gymnastics, after school, Christina preferred to be alone in the solace and safety of her own bedroom. There she began to cope with her anxieties through journaling. As she grew older, Christina learned to cope another way: with humor. Though as a child she could never find the perfect words to express herself in everyday conversation, Christina realized that she excelled in public speaking as she grew up. She learned to use humor to make her audience chuckle during her school presentations, and that put her at ease in front of everyone. Thinking outside the box, she found a way to defeat her fears.

Christina's father always told her, "The difference between possible and impossible is simply the measure of one's will." This taught Christina that her extreme anxiety wasn't a roadblock to her success. It might have been an obstacle, making the journey a bit more challenging than it was for most, but Christina could accomplish her goals with practice, perseverance, and will power.

"Because my father was a straightforward man—did not sugarcoat anything but just said it as it was, even if the truth was harsh—I trusted what he said and his words of wisdom," Christina says. "It was clear to me that as long as I had the will, despite my anxiety and other weaknesses, eventually I would succeed. And I just never gave up until I proved his theory right, time and time again."

Having firsthand experience with the challenges of severe anxiety, Christina decided a career in a helping profession was her calling. She wanted to help others face their difficulties and reach their full potential through the interdependent relationship of mind and body. Christina accepted early admission to McGill University in Montreal, Canada, where she chose to study psychology as her major and exercise science as her minor. Her intention was to use her degrees to create a job for herself, because she did not feel like she fit in to any one career.

Despite the numerous moves in her childhood, Christina was raised mostly in small-town Cornwall, Ontario. Suddenly, she found herself lost in Montreal's sea of people.

Her introductory psychology classes were held in auditoriums with hundreds of students. Christina worried that she would disturb others if she tried to take off her coat and reach into her bag for her notebook. Instead, she tried recording her professor's lectures and absorbing the class content until she could write it down later. But this wasn't enough; Christina needed to see the visuals and be able to ask questions to really learn. Once again, Christina was forced to study extra hard in order to keep up with her classes. Christina persisted and maintained an above-average GPA.

Christina's anxiety affected other aspects of her early-adult life, as well. She was not accustomed to the sheer size of Montreal and chose to avoid crowds of people whenever possible. Instead of taking public transportation home after classes and experiencing what she imagined to be claustrophobia-inducing subways, she often chose to walk an hour and a half, even in the harsh winter weather.

Though Christina struggled daily with her anxiety, an incident on December 5, 1987, would test her limits like nothing before. Christina decided to spend the weekend at home in Cornwall with her parents instead of in her Montreal apartment. That Friday night, she drifted off to sleep, but at two in the morning, she awoke to the wailing of the smoke detector, located on the ceiling just outside her bedroom. As she descended the winding staircase, she started to choke. Thick smoke had filled the interior of the house. Since she had been the first one awakened by the fire alarm, Christina scurried back upstairs to get the rest of the family out of the house. They managed to escape the blaze unharmed, because only half the house had been affected.

Upon completing their investigation, the police determined someone had doused the house with Varsol, a flammable paint thinner, and intentionally set it ablaze. Christina and her family were required to stay elsewhere for the time being. Their house needed repairs, but more importantly, the police told Christina's father that the arsonist might return to finish the job. It was not safe for them to be near their home until further notice.

With Christina and her family relocated to a nearby hotel, an undercover officer hid inside the house for three days in case the arsonist returned. On the third night, the officer concluded the perpetrator would not target the house again, against her father's professional opinion that the arsonist would return. The family was allowed to return to retrieve any belongings they needed for their extended hotel stay. The home would not be livable again until repairs could be made.

That evening, while everyone but one of Christina's sisters was together in the house, the arsonist struck again, and Christina watched as flames ripped through the entire home. The serenity of what had been an ordinary night gave way to total chaos. The roaring fire smashed through the windows and engulfed what was left of the house. Christina ran from her home, sliding and slipping helplessly on the icy road as she observed her safe haven collapse.

After further investigation, the authorities determined both acts of arson were homicide attempts aimed primarily at Christina's father. Given his career as a psychiatrist, authorities suspected he had upset a patient or a patient's family member, and this was an act of retaliation. The police concluded the family was in imminent danger and kept them under strict surveillance at a hotel. Everyone, including Christina and her siblings, was supposed to keep a low profile until authorities were certain their lives were no longer in danger. They were instructed not to leave the hotel room unless absolutely necessary. Christina could not attend classes, and her parents were urged not to go to work. Her mother obeyed, but her father insisted that he could not turn his back on the patients who needed him. Life was at a standstill for a couple months, and Christina was terrified for the safety of her family, especially since the police were never able to arrest anyone related to the arson.

Amid the fear and turmoil of having their house intentionally set ablaze, the family continued to face adversity. Their insurance company refused to pay for the fire damage and subsequent living expenses. The family quickly depleted its bank account as a result of legal fees spent fighting the insurance company, a lengthy hotel stay, and university tuition payments. Because, eventually, neither parent could work during this time, the family had no income.

The aftermath of the house fire placed an enormous strain on Christina's parents. In February 1988, Christina's father decided to leave the family and move to Montreal. Christina was in disbelief and stayed in the hotel with her mother to figure out what to do next. Shortly after their split, both parents fell sick from mental and physical exhaustion and required hospitalization. Though her mother stayed in the hospital for only a week, Christina's father's health began to deteriorate. He had developed lung problems, contracted a virus, suffered a heart attack and a stroke, and battled end-stage pulmonary fibrosis. During this time, Christina cared for both her parents as best as she could.

With already limited funds, the family fell deeper into debt as their bills accumulated. In 1989, Christina, her sister, and her brother were evicted from their condo in Montreal. They were encouraged by family friends to temporarily abandon their education and find jobs instead. They needed a way to support themselves. As beneficial as education would be in the long run, it could not provide for them in the moment. Christina could not receive a student loan because her father's salary from the previous year far exceeded the maximum income allowance for loans, and she couldn't apply for welfare because she didn't have a permanent address. At twenty-one years of age, Christina found herself at a major crossroads.

Christina could have moved back to Cornwall to live with friends and find work at a fast-food chain, but she refused to follow that path. It would have been the safer route, the easier route. But Christina decided that being destitute would not deter her from getting a university education. She was still on a mission to help people, even if that mission had briefly been diverted. Christina, however, missed too much school during her hotel stay and received a "D" average in a vital psychology course. Instead of listening to the advisor who told her she had blown her chance at ever attending graduate school, Christina devised a new plan. She quit McGill and enrolled in another university, hoping to start fresh. She transferred to Concordia University in Montreal. Classes were smaller and included more discussion between the professors and students. Many courses were offered in the evening, so Christina could work during the day.

With nowhere to call home and no money to rent an apartment, Christina slept in public spaces around her new university. When the weather permitted, she camped outside under the stars, and when the temperature dropped, she dragged her sleeping bag into the school's laboratory. When she slept outside, Christina's brother was often with her. They were both afraid, but they were also so exhausted from all the walking and studying that they would fall asleep quickly. When her brother could not be with her, Christina would try to stay awake in an all-night coffee shop; she would then sleep in the daytime in a park and wear a hooded sweatshirt to try to look like a man. When she was unable to stay awake through the night, she would go to a train or bus station, where she would allow herself to doze off from time to time. Christina was scared, but she endured.

With no money for food, Christina frequently wondered where her next meal would come from. Not wanting people at her university to know her situation, she often ate the scraps of food that people left on their mall food-court or fast-food restaurant trays. Her brother would ask people just leaving their tables if he could help them with their trays. He would always choose trays that still had food on them, and instead of taking the trays to the trash can, he would bring the food to another table for him and Christina to eat.

"Most of my belongings were damaged in the fire," Christina says. "Because it was too anxiety-provoking to 'move' to Montreal, I only took bare necessities with me for a week and usually returned to the safety of my home and town on weekends. At school, I had to carry heavy bags with me everywhere: my backpack and bags in both arms. Students could not believe what I toted around on a daily basis, especially considering all the walking I did. I was still wearing my white, woolen winter coat that my sister had used to try to put out flames from the first fire. It smelled like the fire and had black marks all over."

Christina might have lost her possessions, but she still had her will and a strong sense of purpose. She found ways to survive, even when times were trying. Within a year, she earned a job at a group home for adults suffering from mental illness. This job provided her with meals, wages, hot showers, and shelter at night. What it didn't provide, however, was a sense of comfort.

"I never perceived myself as homeless or identified with homelessness," Christina says. "I had found practical solutions surviving on the street and was more terrified to be inside the group home alone at night with the clientele. It was not unusual to be screamed at when I could not give in and give more medication than authorized, or told someone heard voices to hurt me or stab me. I was a petite young adult who looked much younger than my age. They were fourteen middle-aged adults. I had to coach myself before shifts, telling myself that I had faced scary situations in the past and could face the threats that could transpire at work."

Though Christina worked the night shift and was unable to sleep while on the job, she still managed to attend her classes during the day, albeit sleep-deprived.

Despite her exhausting schedule, Christina felt the burdens of the house fire slowly disintegrate. She repeated her mantra in her head: *I have my health. Life is good. And I am blessed.* Christina managed to graduate with honors and even had her thesis published in a psycho-neurophysiology journal. She was forced to work harder than anyone else in her class to graduate, but that was something she had been doing all her life already. To everyone who had thought the effects of the fire would be too much for her to handle, Christina proved she would not be defeated. She had the courage to change her situation by not giving in to her fears and never backing down from the challenges set before her.

Christina's diligence and intelligence did not escape her professors. One even encouraged her to attend graduate school because she needed that level of exposure and education in order to help people the way she was capable of. However, fate dealt another catastrophe into Christina's life, throwing her plan off course. Both her brother and her father suffered heart attacks, and Christina could not turn her back on her family when they needed help most. With all public care facilities filled to capacity and not having the finances to place both her father and brother in a private rehabilitation facility, Christina opted to forgo graduate school and tend to their needs. She cared for her brother for only a few months, but her father required help for a couple of years.

When her family members were well enough for her to leave their sides, Christina sought work in the field of health psychology and behavioral medicine. Having only a bachelor's degree made it difficult to find a job in the field. As she waited for someone to offer her a chance, Christina worked three unrelated jobs to support herself and her family. She never gave up hope, and after nearly nine months of searching, the director of the behavioral medicine department at Concordia offered Christina the opportunity to be his research assistant and coordinator. Christina tried to be honest with this professor about her circumstances, and instead of seeing her obstacles as setbacks, he commended her for all she had achieved despite the difficult scenarios in her life.

From this opportunity, Christina was able to acquire a position working as a research assistant and coordinator for a doctor in a pain management clinic in a hospital. The issue? Christina had, at that time, a strong fear of hospitals. Many mornings before work, Christina could not distract her mind. The anticipation of having to step foot in a hospital ate away at her stomach. The closer she came to her start time, the more her nerves increased. Often, her fear escalated to the point that she ran into the bathroom and vomited. When her fear paralyzed her, Christina recalled her mother saying, "You can do anything you put your mind to." She'd then recall her father saying, "Remember, it is a privilege to help people." Christina summoned her courage, just as she had been doing her entire life, held her head high, and walked through the doors of her hospital.

Christina's lack of graduate education never deterred her from growing in her field. When she began working at the hospital, she learned that if she wanted to excel in her field, she needed to gain as much knowledge and clinical experience as possible. The focus needed to be on her skills, not her education or pay. Because she held some national coaching certifications and had coached gymnastics in her teen years, Christina would volunteer to fill the spot of a physiotherapist with a gentle stretch class when patients were stuck without an activity. She also agreed to go back to McGill University at nights and on weekends for further certification in exercise so she could help even more. She did this without earning extra pay.

By the time the doctor who hired her retired from his clinic twelve years later, insurance companies had pleaded with Christina to continue to provide rehabilitative services to better serve their needs and the needs of their clients. Many other doctors discouraged her from doing so because it required a steep financial backing and many more educational credentials than she had. Yet again, Christina went against the current and opened her own rehabilitation center to come to the aid of patients such as injured workers and victims of automobile accidents. Christina created a thriving facility for pain treatment and research: the CAP Pain Centre. The facility became synonymous with success, and it was even cited in *Canadian Living* magazine. Insurance companies would fly patients great distances just to attend the CAP Pain Centre because its rehabilitation plans proved to be more successful than conventional clinics. Where those clinics failed to heal, Christina's clinic succeeded.

At the age of forty, Christina finally had built the life she'd always wanted. She was helping people, running (and owning) a successful clinic, and no longer worrying about finances. Christina had reached a point where she could finally imagine settling down and starting her own family. She was ready for the next great chapter in her life.

"I had performed beyond my expectations and reached a level of success I never dreamed of," Christina says. "When I had come up with a program and a well-trained team of professionals that was effective in getting people's lives back in work, love, and play, I felt it was time to find my own balance in those areas, the life I had been dreaming of. I certainly had found the recipe to achieve it, I just had to apply it for myself."

Then, her father's pulmonary fibrosis became critical, and Christina's world spun faster than ever. She continued to run her clinic during the day without lessening her work-load—her schedule was filled to the brim with meetings, overseeing her staff of twelve, and monitoring patients. She would leave work for lunch and supper to feed her father. She kept telling herself to be a solider and just do every-thing. When her father's condition worsened and he needed to be intubated, Christina sat at his bedside in the ICU, often arriving home around ten at night. She was beyond exhausted. Her body begged her to slow down and care for herself, too. Overall, she was not feeling physically well. Her immune system weakened and she caught every illness that was spreading. Even when she wasn't sick, she never woke up feeling refreshed and rejuvenated. But instead of heeding her body's warning immediately, Christina kept up her feverish pace. Her weakened physical state required her to push even harder to accomplish less. She figured she would rest and focus on her own needs as soon as her father was well. In the meantime, however, she continued down the path of unintentional self-destruction without really worrying about the consequences.

A week after her father moved into a rehabilitation center, Christina knew the time for self-care had come. She began by drawing a hot, relaxing bath filled with Epsom salts and calming essential oils. As she let her body sink deeper into the water, she felt her tensions begin to release. Slowly, the steaming water and lavender scents erased the worry that had been lingering on her mind. Christina surrendered to the soothing bath and understood just how badly she had needed it. She rubbed lavender oil on her temples until her head felt light enough to float away. She then massaged her neck, which had held a large portion of her tension. When her muscle tightness gave way, she moved down further. As she rubbed the oils over her breasts, Christina froze.

"Within a millisecond, it felt like millions of pieces of shattered glass were suddenly poking into every single nerve in my body…I sat up abruptly and gasped. I knew in the pit of my stomach that what I felt in my chest was not good, that I was in a state of dis-ease," she explains. "A bizarre feeling overcame me: a heaviness on my head and shoulders, and a strange chiseling sensation in my tightened face. I felt myself turn into stone while parts of me were being chipped away. I went numb."

Christina had found a lump in her breast, and it didn't feel like the harmless cysts she had noticed in the past.

After unsuccessfully trying to rid her breast of the lump with castor oil, Christina went to her doctor for an expert opinion. After a mammogram and ultrasound, her doctor recommended a biopsy; there was no other way to know whether the cells were benign or malignant.

Time stopped for Christina as she awaited the biopsy results, her anxiety in full force. She sat in the waiting room unable to focus on anything except her breast. The knots in her stomach wound tighter and tighter as the minutes passed. She watched in anticipation as the doctor walked by the doorway time and again, moving on to every other patient. She studied his face for any clues each time she noticed him. She learned nothing. Finally, unable to sit still any longer, she paced the room trying to rid her mind of the intense fear that gripped it. Walking in circles was not the panacea she hoped it would be. Instead, she started to hyperventilate.

After five hours, Christina was called back to the exam room. The time had come to learn the prognosis. The doctor confirmed what Christina had already subconsciously known: cancer.

According to the Breast Cancer Society of Canada, one in every eight Canadian women will develop breast cancer. The time had come for Christina to accept that she was the one. She did not, however, wish to be the Canadian Cancer Society's statistical one out of every thirty-one Canadian women who lose their lives to breast cancer. She immediately scheduled a partial mastectomy for two weeks later.

Prepping for surgery that day, Christina knew very well there were two possible outcomes with the malignant cells her doctor was about to remove: 1) the cells would be contained to the breast only, or 2) the cells had spread to her lymph nodes, which would mean a much more extensive treatment process. As she drifted off to anesthetic-induced slumber, Christina focused on the former outcome.

In the recovery room, Christina woke to her doctor's voice confirming that the cancerous cells were found only in the breast. Her doctor had removed the malignancies and her breast remained in near-perfect condition aside from a minuscule incision from the surgery.

When the doctor came in, "I was terrified and asked for his hand," Christina remembers. "When he told me my nodes were negative and the cancer contained, I cried. I had been so blessed, and I knew I would be okay from there. I fell back to sleep but was awakened by the nurse prying my hand from the surgeon's to let him go for his next surgery."

Though the cancer had not shown signs of spreading, the medical staff determined Christina should undergo chemotherapy because of her young age. Her cancer conquest had not yet been completed. Christina underwent sixteen weeks of intravenous chemotherapy treatment and an additional year of intravenous immunotherapy. Though the staff at the facility remained positive and lifted her spirits, Christina withdrew from the world whenever she could. The chemotherapy caused her to lose her hair. The steroids caused her to eat nonstop. She was balding and gaining weight and preferred to avoid her reflection. Neither the person she saw in the mirror nor the person she heard in her head was the self Christina knew.

Not only did Christina have to find a way to accept the person she had become while undergoing chemotherapy, she also had to find a way to tune out everyone else's negative experiences with cancer. When you have cancer, everybody around you knows it, and they want to share their experience with the disease even if it is discouraging—and whether you want them to or not. Christina's mood after finishing her final dose of chemo instantly changed from ecstatic to solemn after a run-in with someone at her condo complex. Though he meant well by sharing the story of how his brother had lost his battle with cancer, Christina wanted nothing more than to crawl under her covers and hide from the world. She was taking all the proper steps and precautions to fight this disease, and his story reminded Christina of the possibility that none of it might matter in the end.

During this trying time, Christina learned of a family link to breast cancer. She had become acquainted with two distant cousins in Greece who were both losing their battles with breast cancer. Doctors informed all three women, Christina included, on separate occasions that there was no genetic predisposition to this type of cancer in their family. Yet here she was, losing two of her cousins to the killer disease.

Christina was determined she would not become another statistic. In February 2009, five months after her diagnosis, she underwent a preventative double mastectomy and immediate breast reconstruction.

This decision did not come easily. While searching for photos of breast cancer survivors who had chosen the mastectomy/reconstruction combination, Christina found nothing but headless torsos. These women were treated as subjects rather than humans. The photographs showed the medical journey of breast reconstruction, but Christina wanted to see the human journey: the women behind the surgeries, the happiness after the trials. Christina searched for the reassurance that these women still considered themselves to be beautiful, confident, and sexy—even with their reconstructed breasts. When she could not find that reassurance, she wept in her father's arms.

In her book, *Harmony after Breast Cancer and Reconstruction*, Christina explains how raw and vulnerable she felt in that moment. "When I couldn't cry anymore, I confided in [my father] my many secret fears: that I might die young, like my cousins, and alone; that I may never be able to have children; that my partner might not find me attractive anymore, leave me, or worse, stay with me out of guilt; that no one would ever want to look at me again, not even myself in the mirror."

Christina's father reminded her that "illness is a part of life and life itself is not to be feared." This gave Christina the courage she needed to move forward with the double mastectomy and breast reconstruction. This was her promise to her cousins: to beat breast cancer, to survive. Christina concluded the best way to do that was to eliminate the risk of malignant cells ever returning to the breast.

While the loss of her favorite feminine assets bothered Christina, she woke from her double mastectomy relieved and renewed. She would eventually have implants surgically placed, and her feeling of femininity would return. First, she had to endure eight months of discomfort provided by the tissue expanders placed under the muscles and skin in her chest. These devices would slowly expand, allowing the muscles and skin to grow, so that one day implants could be added. Christina lived with a constant feeling of pressure and stretching in her chest; however, this discomfort reminded Christina that she was cancer-free. And that was a reason to be grateful.

Christina received her implants, one of the final stages of her breast reconstruction, eight months after the mastectomy. Throughout her entire ordeal, Christina wished she had found photographs of whole, smiling women who had undergone the same procedures. Instead she found those headless torsos. She knew that women in her situation needed to be confident in their mastectomy decisions. They needed to find photographs that illustrated how life on the other side of breast reconstruction could be just as happy and carefree as before. These women needed to see proof that they would feel confident in their appearance again, that reminders of their breast cancer would not be lurking in their life forever. Many times at her doctor's office, Christina would meet women who were struggling with the decision to have a mastectomy. When these women found out Christina had undergone the entire process, they asked if they could see her breasts in private. The first time someone asked to see her reconstructed breasts, Christina was hesitant to show a complete stranger such a personal part of her body. But after a moment of thought, she realized she had the power to encourage. These women needed visible reassurance that they were making the right choice. When they saw Christina's reconstructed breasts, their expressions changed from frightened to relieved. Tears filled their eyes, and each time Christina knew she had found a bright spot in her cancer journey. Her experiences allowed her to offer help to other women just starting their own paths.

This prompted Christina to act on a larger level. With the help of her best friend and a photographer, Christina decided to create her own photographic journey of the female figure post-breast reconstruction. They launched the Shirts Off for Breast Reconstruction Initiative and created the photo-intense book *Harmony after Breast Cancer and Reconstruction*. This book includes photos of Christina post-reconstructive surgery and an inspirational narrative about life after breast cancer. Her bravery and candor in the book allows women to understand the journey of breast cancer in its entirety. Christina shows how emotional turmoil comes with the diagnosis. Many women fear that having a mastectomy and reconstruction will leave them feeling less feminine or attractive, but Christina proves otherwise with this book.

She writes, "If you think that getting a mastectomy is the end of feeling feminine and sexy, it is just the beginning...I know for sure that the breasts I have now opened the most important door ever—the door to the rest of my beautiful and more meaningful life when sexy is something that emanates from the inside out."

Christina Anston is a woman who has faced multiple challenges throughout her life and has persisted each time. She was taught never to back down, so she learned to tackle her crippling anxiety, challenged those who said she couldn't, and fought for what she wanted even when the odds were stacked against her. Her constant willingness to fight her battles, even when they appeared too grave, is an inspiring example of fortitude that deserves admiration and emulation.

"My life challenges up to the diagnosis at forty had taught me how to survive; however, it was breast cancer that taught me to live," Christina recounts. "Yes, I struggled, and yes, I had been terrified, insecure, anxious, and afraid. But aren't those all the ingredients for one to want to make things better? These and my desire to help others have been the propellers, the fuel pushing my will and desire to succeed, to show the world that everything is possible. No fear is worth losing your dreams over. Nothing is impossible when you believe, and that I do. I believe."

. . . .

If you'd like to support a cause close to Christina's heart, please visit the Canadian Cancer Society's BRA Day program at bra-day.com.

References

Alcoholics Anonymous. www.aa.org. Accessed 5 July 2018.

Anston, Christina. *Harmony after Breast Cancer and Reconstruction.* CAP, Inc., 2018.

Breast Cancer Society of Canada. bcsc.ca. Accessed 5 July 2018.

"Breast Cancer Statistics." *Canadian Cancer Society*, www.cancer.ca/en/cancer-information/cancer-type/breast/statistics/?region=on. Accessed 5 July 2018.

Cicero, Theodore J., Ph.D., and Matthew S. Ellis, MPE, and Hilary L. Surratt, Ph.D. "The Changing Face of Heroin Use in the United States." *JAMA Psychiatry*, Vol. 71, No. 7, 2014, pp. 821-826.

"Fighting Opioid Overdose." *Centers for Disease Control and Prevention.* April 2017, www.cdc.gov/features/fighting-opioid-overdose/index.html. Accessed 5 July 2018.

Gage, Nicholas and Eleni Gatzoyiannis. *Eleni.* Collins, 1983.

Geiling, Natasha. "Before the Revolution." *Smithsonian.com*, 31 July 2007, www.smithsonianmag.com/history/before-the-revolution-159682020/. Accessed 5 July 2018.

Geraldi, Camille and Carol Burris. *Camille's Children: 31 Miracles and Counting.* Andrews McMeel Publishing, 1996.

"Heroin." *Center for Substance Abuse Research*, www.cesar.umd.edu/cesar/drugs/heroin.asp. Accessed 5 July 2018.

Pacenti, John. "Hate Drives Big-hearted family from Home." *SouthCoastToday.com*, 25 January 1997 and updated 10 January 2011, http://www.southcoasttoday.com/article/19970125/LIFE/301259999. Accessed 5 July 2018.

"Stressed Cells/AARP/Camille/The Awful Truth." *60 Minutes Wednesday,* executive produced by Jeffrey Fager, Columbia Broadcasting System, 2005.

Strong, Faith. *The Glories of Sobriety.* New Directions for Women, 2009.